GHERARDO ORTALLI
GIOVANNI SCARABELLO

A SHORT HISTORY
of VENICE

PACINIeditore

English translation by
Amanda Mazzinghi

CONTENTS

The "Venetia" that preceded Venice

For all of us today Venice is essentially a city: one tends to see her as the expression, perhaps the highest expression, of the nearest we can get to the ideal city. But in spite of this, in spite of her intrinsic qualities and in spite of the way we now see things, the history of Venice was for a long time the history of a city that did not exist. "Venetia", together with Istria, was simply one of the regions (the tenth) into which the Emperor Augustus had divided the northern and central part of the Italian peninsula. From this, the original Venetian unit, extending from the Alps to the Adriatic sea, from Istria to the River Oglio (and indeed the Adda) a second Venice was to emerge, composed of lagoons rather than dry land, of islands and lidos scattered between the mouths of the Isonzo and the Po: from Grado to Cavarzere, as the documents of *la Serenissima* (the Most Serene) Republic of Venice were to define it.

The process by which the old, mainland (or *terraferma*) "Venetia" distinguished itself from the new, maritime "Venetia" was started by external factors connected with the dramatic events that followed the Longobard invasion which in 569 engulfed a Byzantine Italy ill prepared to contain it. Much the same thing had happened already in the middle of the fifth century, when, in the forays of the Huns led by

Attila (and before that in the Visigoth invasions), the lagoons had offered a tolerably safe refuge to the peoples of the *terraferma* fleeing before an unstoppable enemy.

In those disastrous events, however, the balance between the two parts of the area had not really altered; above all, there had been no steady increase in the population or functions of the lagoons. The Attilan tempest had really blown over fairly rapidly; the invaders' raids brought tragic destruction but no lasting changes to the area. The refugees in the lagoons were able to return to the places they came from, without serious impediment to the resumption of their old way of life.

Things were to go differently with the Longobard incursions. This time invasion meant the violent migration of an entire population which entered Italy with the firm intention of staying there, so that for the peoples who from the *terraferma* cities – from Padua or Altino to Oderzo, Concordia or Aquileia – retreated to the lagoons, waiting for the storm to pass, the way back was closed. The first step in the building of a different Venice, the first actions that suggest the shaping of a new situation which would, in the end, revolutionise the balance of forces throughout the area, was informed by the negative spirit of the refugee, whose mind is turned back to a past which he cannot believe has gone for good, a past to which he intends to return as soon as the emergency is over. The defence of the old, pre-Longobard world, which he was determined to see as a plausible model even though it was well and truly dead, became the reason for the birth of the new world: civilisation and the Venetian state, with whatever subversive and innovative qualities it had room for. There was more to this process than the apparent paradox that the story of Venice seems, but only seems, to present.

The Longobard presence, which, rather than weakening, gradually eroded the area remaining in Byzantine hands, would eventually have reached the margins of the lagoons, completing the transformation of the ancient *terraferma* Venice. But this second, new, maritime Venice was not yet a city and would not assume her essential characteristics until the ninth century.

The myth of creation from nothing

What the initial situation was, and what the areas in which the new Venice took shape looked like, are recorded for us in the letter which the prefect of the praetorium, Cassiodorus, sent in 537 - 538 to the local maritime tribunes. It was necessary to organise the rapid transport of goods from Istria to the capital, Ravenna, but this highly placed official (the Goth Vitige ruled in Italy at that time) did not limit himself to a dry bureaucratic note; he wrote a letter of outstanding literary quality, dwelling at length on a careful description that is still in some ways valid today.

It tells us about men accustomed to limitless spaces, capable of getting about even while storms raged over the sea, by using that network of routes through the lagoons by which boats seem almost to be gliding over fields, when in reality the seabed of the channels is hidden from the onlooker by islands and sandbanks. The soil is continually submerged and uncovered again by the alternating tides. The scattered houses, built on land shored up by bundles of pliant withies, look like waders' nests. Boats are tied up to their walls, like domestic animals. Poverty lives alongside riches, on equal terms, nourished by the same food, sheltered by the same sort of house; there is no envy of family glory. The only abundance lies in fish, and, there being no place for ploughs or sickles, whatever else is needed in the way of food is purchased with salt.

Cassiodorus's description undoubtedly justifies its studied rhetoric. The climate of virtuous equality and social peace, the exaltation of a simple and industrious way of life answer to stereotypical models of the time, but behind them we glimpse the realities of the age. This was a way of life built upon territory that demands constant effort to consolidate it, a life lived in marsh dwellings that were for the most part rather simple and scattered, a society organised by hardworking people engaged in maritime jobs, that is to say in fisheries and salt-works. Social organisation must have been on the whole pretty homogeneous at pretty low levels, but it nevertheless allowed the development of something higher. In any case, the area was a part of the organisational system (both political and territorial) which belonged to Roman tradition; it was most certainly not uninhabited or abandoned, as the mythical story of the origins of Venice claims.

According to this story, the creation of Venice from nothing, like the birth of Venus from the sea, was the achievement of free peoples who fled from barbarian invaders to desert islands. The story was concocted for very practical reasons, and so well concocted that it is still accepted as the truth even now. The Venetians, including their most powerful rulers, had an interest in believing a tale of this sort. To hold that the islands where Venice came into being had never known an earlier form of settlement or social life was equivalent to affirming that Venice had always been independent. If there had been nothing there, then there had been no subordination or servitude either; the myth of coming from nothing makes that of the original liberty of Venice plausible and much more important politically.

The legend was therefore the basis and the reflection of an ideological and political programme destined to withstand any claim made by any external authority.

The foundations of the new Venice

Even if the islands of the lagoon region were not uninhabited and wild, as the myth claims, the process set in motion by the Longobard invasion turned out all the same to be profoundly innovative, destined to upset the existing order of things throughout the upper Adriatic area. That lagoon area was undoubtedly marginal in the Roman era (and whether it was poorly or splendidly marginal makes no essential difference) but it came to assume a special centrality. In other words, it is only in legend that Venice appeared suddenly: her true birth took many centuries of slow progress towards a new balance of characteristics, a progress set off, as we have said, in 569 when various different peoples fled to the islands of the lagoon region from the Longobard peril.

In this population shift, all the layers of *terraferma* society were involved and the characteristics of each were preserved. These people were not destitute refugees who came to new terrain to build a new society; on the contrary, they were people of various social levels, who brought with them their various rights, functions and social roles. Chief among them were the leading members of their ecclesiastical hierarchy, including its chief representative, the patriarch of Aquileia. When he took refuge in Grado he brought with him the treasures of his Church, not only material wealth but also spiritual treasures, and first and foremost among them precious relics. The influx of refugees continued for a long time. Wave after wave arrived as the Longobards gradually took new areas of territory from the Byzantines, until 639 when, with the fall of Oderzo, the provincial seat of civil and military administration, the old Byzantine defensive system collapsed and almost all the Venetian *terraferma* was lost to the Empire. This was a key moment in the emergence of the new, maritime Venice. Cittanova/Eraclea, on the edge of the lagoon region, became the regional capital, while the ancient Roman municiple centres (such as Aquileia or Concordia or Altino) entered on a phase of acute crisis and finally disappeared.

The dedication stone of the new church of Santa Maria on the island of Torcello testifies to the changes that took place. The stone can still be seen in the basilica. It is dated 639, the year in which Oderzo fell, and the founders who are named are the highest authorities in Byzantine Italy: first the exarch, then the "magister militum", military commander of the Venetian region on behalf of the Empire, and finally Bishop Mauro who, having fled from Altino to the lagoons, is traditionally considered to have been the first Bishop of Torcello. The lay and ecclesiastical authorities joined forces here in an action, of great moral significance, which encouraged the reorganisation of life in the lagoon region during the very same months in which the last bastions fell in the *terraferma* region.

Towards autonomy, under Byzantine colours

The new, maritime Venice eluded the grasp of the Longobards. It continued to be a part of the Byzantine empire as a dependent province of the exarch ruling from Ravenna, who in turn came directly under the Constantinople government. The "magister militum" headed the administration of the lagoon province, both civil and military but principally the latter. All local powers were vested in the tribunes, who were responsible to him. The tribunes were drawn from the class that provided the riches underpinning Venice. They were in this sense the aristocracy, and for a long time, together with the ecclesiastical hierarchy, they furnished the framework of public organisation.

Naturally all public administration was carried out in the name of the Byzantine government, to which all administrators were officially loyal, but the very difficult times had brought about certain changes. The war against the Longobards dragged on and this meant that the predominance of the military role over the civil in public administration became a permanent condition, to such an extent that society in the lagoon province could be said to have become militarised. The Byzantine empire was hard pressed on many fronts and had great difficulty in sending troops to areas which grew ever more distant from central government. Constantinople had to count more and more on local administrations, and this inevitably encouraged the development of a stronger and stronger tendency towards independence.

People have seen, often naively, the figure of the Doge as a symbol of independence from Byzantium, beginning with that mythical first Doge Paulicius who in about 713-716 took the place of the Byzantine "magistri militum." The fact is that even the position of Doge (or "dux" or duke) was a Byzantine office and does not in itself indicate any acquired independence. A more significant step on the road to autonomy came at the time of the iconoclastic row that broke out when the Byzantine Emperor Leo III Isauricus condemned the cult of images, taking a religious position that was strongly contested by the Pope. In the resulting conflict between Rome and Byzantium which began in 726-727 there were serious clashes in Italy. The Venetian troops and those of the Pentapoli (roughly corresponding to today's Marche) mutinied, joining forces with the Pope and refusing the authority of the exarch. They placed themselves under the authority of leaders chosen without reference to the central government. So, with this military gesture and the election of Duke Orso, Venice for the first time indicated autonomously who should lead her, but this did not in any way signify that she had left the Byzantine world. On the contrary. Once the period of extreme difficulty had passed and harmony had been restored, Orso continued in leadership with approval from his superiors. In any case, with the Longobard king Liutprandus threatening the frontiers, any dangerous rupture would have been too risky. However, from that moment onwards (apart from the brief return to "magistri militum" between 737 and about 742) the Doge was in practice accepted as the ruler of Venice, except by Constantinople.

The fact that Venice thereafter loosened the ties of her political dependence more and more was not too much of a problem for the Empire. There were advantages in the situation for both parties. For the people of the lagoons, dependence on rulers who became ever more distant and ever less able to interfere concretely in local life meant seeking shelter independence upon other powers, the Longobards or, later, the Franks or the Saxon emperors. They were nearer, but they too were dangerous, though in quite other ways. At the same time, continued dependence on Constantinople also meant remaining an integral part of the Byzantine economic system, which was rich in exceptional opportunities and contacts compared with that of the European west, which was depressed and underdeveloped. From the Byzantine point of view, maintaining the bond with the lagoons guaranteed a presence in zones of great economic and strategic importance. (Remember: the northern part of the Adriatic is the point at which the waters of the Mediterranean basin push up northward towards the heart of the European continent.)

Basically, maintaining the bond with the lagoon region assured a political role otherwise impossible for the Byzantines, pressed as they were by more urgent demands in other areas of military operation.

All this became more evident after 751 when King Astolfus with his Longobards entered a defeated Ravenna. The exarch was taken prisoner and the whole Byzantine system in northern and central Italy collapsed without hope of recovery. At that point, Venice's movement towards independence underwent an inevitable acceleration, but the problems were by no means over. Other dangerous actors appeared on the scene.

After the Longobards, the Franks

The dominion of the exarch having fallen, the Pope found himself confronted by the Longobards, whose hegemonic claims on Italy were by now on the point of being realised. Assessing realistically the uselessness of counting on a Byzantine recovery, he made a new, solid concordat, allying himself with the Frankish kingdom. As a result of this agreement with Rome, Charlemagne conquered the Longobard kingdom in 774, but for Venice the new neighbour was more to be feared than his predecessor. The Carolingian Emperor made no secret of his desire to acquire every scrap of Byzantine territory to be found in regions that were by now solidly Frankish. There now opened an extremely delicate phase, in which the problems of foreign policy were interwoven with the internal tensions between those in Venice who were more alert to the opportunities offered by the sea and commerce (and who therefore preferred to look towards the east for allies) and those who, on the contrary, identified themselves with traditional interests in land. A pro-Frankish party thus came to oppose a pro-Byzantine party. The antagonism between the two led to the loyalist Doges Giovanni and Maurizio II Falbaio (both of them involved in the murder of the patriarch of Grado, who had allied himself to the papal and Frankish positions) being deposed and replaced by the pro-Frankish Obelerius and Beatus in 803.

Venice was, indeed, all but conquered, in a brief period of Carolingian domination during which the lagoon territory was occupied by the troops of Charlemagne's son, King Pipino. However, at this decisive moment Byzantine arms returned for the last time, and the eastern fleet proved to be the crucial factor. What it came to was that Charlemagne attached more importance to Byzantium's recognition of the title of Emperor, conferred upon him by the Pope at Christmas in the year 800, than to supremacy in the lagoon area. Venice, therefore, remained Byzantine and, to consolidate this new balance of power, the pro-Frank Doges Obelerius and Beatus went into exile, their place taken by Agnello Particiaco, who was unquestionably loyal to Byzantium.

The moment proved to have been critical. In those years, spanning the late eighth and early ninth centuries, Venice had been nearer than ever before to being swallowed up in a unified, feudal *terraferma* region, and this would have drawn her away from the very things she had a propensity to. The lagoon province was already becoming known as the hinge connecting different worlds, a bridge between the European west and the Islamic and Byzantine areas in the east. It was a function for which she was well fitted. Through the city there passed continually Tyrean purple and other richly dyed stuffs from the east, together with valuable leathers and costly spices; untreated skins, iron and timber for building, much in demand in Islamic countries; and the raw materials which Byzantium and the Saracens bought in exchange for valuable finished products. The interchange was not unlike that between the developed and developing countries today. One sure source of profit was the slave trade. From time to time it was banned, but this did not stop it, indeed the recurrent prohibitions made it more lucrative. All this was combined with the transport of people and goods, third-party commerce and the small-scale coasting trade which had always gone on along the upper Adriatic coasts. Commerce of all these kinds was to become more clearly defined as time went on.

The Byzantine return in 810 was also marked by a new change of capital. After the change from Oderzo to Eraclea/Cittanova in 639, there was another from Eraclea to Malamocco in 742, when the last period of government by "magistri militum" came to an end in the lagoon region. Malamocco was in an area that was much more secure militarily, and Agnello Particiaco, once the Frankish threat had passed, transferred his political and administrative headquarters to the group of linked Rialto islands which remained forever central to the life of the Serenissima. (Rialto was at that date the name not simply of a part of the market but of the whole complex of islands.) Particiaco moved his own residence to the place where the Ducal Palace is still to be found, overlooking the San Marco basin. Before long the relics of St Mark were moved from there to the chapel of the palace. (Merchants had spirited them away to Alexandria, in Egypt, in 828.) The rapid building of the basilica to house them re-inforced the role of the Rialto islands as the unquestioned fulcrum of the Doge's government, both civil and religious.

The translation of the evangelist's body and the promotion of his cult were, to tell the truth, more the outcome of a political operation than a response to spiritual demands. The relics arrived promptly when it was necessary to parry the blow sustained at the synod of Mantua in 827, at which, in the presence of papal and imperial legates, the Italic bishops proclaimed the spiritual subordination of Grado (that is to say, the subordination of the church of the lagoon area which regarded the patriarch of Grado as its head) to Aquileia, a patriarchal see of the *terraferma* region, near to and in harmony with the political authorities of the Italic kingdom. These authorities were unconnected with the independence of Venetian ways and often antagonistic to them. It was a dangerous step: any ecclesiastical subordination (especially in view of the leading role played by religious institutions in the society of that time) would have opened the way to other kinds of subordination. Venice therefore responded in an extremely cunning way, which was able to awaken deep resonances in the collective sensibility. A great beating of drums heralded the arrival of the remains of St Mark, founder of the church at Aquileia, whose name had been heard so many times in the deliberations of the synod in Mantua. And his cult, with which the Doge's government had identified itself, was triumphantly established: St Mark was from that time treated as the symbol of the spiritual unity of Venice, fulcrum of a national church that reflected every sort of impulse towards independence.

The years in which the Doge established himself at Rialto and the relics of St. Mark found a worthy resting place in an ever more splendid basilica were the years in which another, a new Venice began to come into being. After centuries of Venice the *terraferma* region and Venice the lagoon region, Venice began to be also the city we recognise today, but for centuries she was in addition (indeed more commonly) known as "civitas Rivoalti", the city of Rialto.

Today we see the second decade of the ninth century as important in the city's development, but in the eyes of contemporaries the beginning of the tenth was a crucial moment. It was in the time of Pietro Tribuno, when the Magyar horsemen, the scourge of the Almighty, who were devastating the whole of Europe with their raids and massacres, made their appearance in the lagoon region. For protection against their incursions a wall was built to connect Santa Maria Zobenigo (Santa Maria of the Lily) with the ancient castle of Olivolo, in the area still known as the Castello, where since about 775 a bishop's see had been established. The walls enclosed the side of the Rialto islands that was most vulnerable, owing to the presence of the main centres of political and ecclesiastical life; the strong chain of iron stretched across Canal Grande, between Santa Maria del Giglio and San Gregorio, to control the access of ships and mercantile landing places completed the defensive measures which conferred unity and solidarity on the inhabited nucleus of the city.

Venice had had centres of civil and military government for some time, but this latest action finally gave her the characteristic which to medieval man was essential to a city: a system of walls. And so it was possible to declare that "the Doge Pietro Tribuno together with his people began to build a city at Rialto." This is round about the year 900, and we can truly say, however naive it may seem, that the statement may be regarded as the birth certificate of the city of Venice.

Between Saracens and Slavs: the difficulties of the ninth century

The Magyar raids, which had acted as midwife to the new "civitas", were followed by a period that was fairly peaceful for Venice. The middle years of the ninth century were much worse, owing above all to the internal difficulties which accompanied the consolidation of the institutions of the Doge's government. Chief among these difficulties were the shifting balances of power between the most important families, which made the Doge's power unstable. The tribunal class (which was to disappear before the end of the century) brought an added precariousness to the situation. It too was a class whose interests were better served by a non-centralised administration of public affairs. All this instability militated against the consolidation of those powers vested in the person of the Doge that had been in effect for some time.

Consequently a change at the top often happened in a traumatic way, with the dismissal of the then Doge in office. Usually he was sent to some monastery (if they were prepared to have him), and this was an improvement on the treatment meeted out to the first Doges. With them it was customary to gouge out their eyes, according to a custom which perhaps indicates certain cultural connections (using "culture" in the widest sense), reminding us as it does of the typically oriental delight in mutilation and other horrible forms of punishment.

If problems were not lacking in the internal politics of the ninth century, external affairs produced the greatest achievements, above all at sea. The less effective and more intermittent Byzantine presence in the Adriatic; insurrections in the Balkans and Slav expansion with the arrival of raiders dedicated to piracy on the Dalmation coasts (especially around the mouth of the Neretva); the spread of the Saracens further and further north, especially after they had begun the conquest of Sicily (in 827), the sacking of Brindisi, the occupation of Taranto and, in 847, the establishment of an emirate at Bari – all these new conditions and the advent of new and dangerous foes rendered the Adriatic unsafe, and it was indispensable for Venice to keep the Adriatic open if she did not wish to be restricted to the lagoons. So from 827-828 when the Doge of that time, Justinian Particiaco, sent a fleet against the Saracens at the request of Byzantium, a long and often painful phase opened, in which Venice made every effort to block the enemy's counter-offensives, which extended right up to the city's inshore waters, with the Slavs reaching as far as Caorle (in about 846) and the Saracens reaching Grado (in 875).

For more than half a century, from about 880, these efforts stretched her capacities to the utmost. The blows she received outnumbered her successes (at least until about 850); nevertheless, whatever the contingent fortunes or misfortunes of those years, Venice achieved great things. The first was the very fact of managing to weather the harsh times without crumbling; better still, she had been able to avoid being bottled up, to maintain the freedom of the Adriatic sea; she had succeeded in performing a role which by now made her a player on the international political scene. Her part may not yet have been comparable with those of the great powers, but it could not be called small or local.

Her final achievement was extremely important: at the end of all this the Doge's government emerged, almost completely, from subordination to Byzantium; without endangering the old bonds, which were useful to her, and without any spectacular – and unprofitable – show of rebellion, the path towards autonomy had reached a point at which, beyond any formal dependence, the relation of Venice to the Byzantine Empire was more like the loyalty of an old ally than the submission of a subject.

Half a century of peace, until the Candian squall and the Turks

When Giovanni II Particiaco became Doge in 881, half a century of political tranquillity began, which favoured substantial development. A *modus vivendi* had been reached with the Slavs, underpinned by the payment of tribute. This was no loss of honour, considering how profitable the money invested in this way was, in terms of peace and commercial security, and if the piracy practised by the people of the coasts settled by Slavs is regarded not as a violation of fundamental rights and principles, however valid, but more realistically as one type of economy that could not be hindered without being replaced by others. As for the Saracens, the place they acquired in a more stable international central Mediterranean system simplified things to such an extent that after 872-875 there were no further clashes; and when, in Pietro II Orsolo's time, in 1002-1003, fighting again broke out, it was Venice's turn to be the aggressor. And even with Byzantium, as with the west, life went on smoothly.

Although there were some difficult moments, on the whole the situation allowed Venetian institutions to grow stronger and stronger. One such moment was that of the Magyar raids, which we mentioned earlier; worse still were the events of 887, when the bellicose young Pietro I Candiano was appointed Doge. He threw himself at once into attacking the Slavs of Neretva, an action which ended tragically with his death. This must have caused great distress to the Venetians, who brought his remains home and buried them in the Grado basilica. But on the whole these were small disturbances in an otherwise steady trend towards improvement. This is all the more striking when one compares what was happening to Venice with what was happening all over the post-Carolingian Empire and the violent turmoil that was rocking the Italic kingdom.

The generally speaking peaceful climate allowed positive developments in a period which was nevertheless hard. The level of life, even in the most prosperous places, was terribly low by present-day standards. The calm that reigned in those decades gave no hint of the storms that were to break out in the course of the tenth century, during the Candiano era. The family that had already produced Pietro I, who died in 887, went on to produce three other Doges who governed Venice almost without interruption from 932 to 976 and who, besides viewing the position of Doge as dynastic, left their mark on those years in a series of energetic initiatives.

With them the hegemony which prevailed

in the Adriatic, north of the Pola-Ravenna line, was accompanied by involvement in what was going on in the *terraferma* region to an extent that produced quarrels within the family itself. The most dramatic moments arrived with Pietro IV Candiano, whose political line was characterised by marked attention to the feudal west, demonstrated on many significant occasions. For instance, having abandoned his first wife (setting her up honourably as abbess of the convent of San Zaccaria), he married into the finest aristocracy of the Italic peninsula in the person of Waldrada, daughter of the Marquess Uberto of Tuscany; he recruited mercenary troops in the *terraferma* region – an unheard-of thing – and they defended him to the end; he introduced the feudal type of social organisation into the lagoon region, where the relationship of vassal and lord had never taken root, since the lack of land was unsuited to it; and he sent Venetian troops to fight in *terraferma* territory they were not accustomed to, such as Ferrara and Oderzo.

These actions serve to measure Candiano's impulse to yield to the pull from the west, expressed in a policy that in the end aroused such opposition that there was a violent uprising in 976. Pietro IV was murdered together with his little son and their bodies were displayed in the public slaughter-house, in the part of Rialto that was becoming the centre of commercial and mercantile business; it was a gesture which indicated tragically the end of a political programme that had not succeeded in modifying the ways in which Venice traditionally viewed her role as hinge between east and west. It was not the end, however, of the period of danger for the lagoon region.

The principal dangers came from the interest which the Empire, reborn in the west under the skilful guidance of Otto I and still more Otto II, of the House of Saxony, took in the Venetian areas. Otto II's open warfare against the lagoon state was very hard to withstand and was hindered only by the unexpected death of the Emperor. The men of the time chose to see in this death the direct intervention of divine providence. It had been prophesied by the great abbot of Cluny, Maiolo.

Pietro II Orseolo and the characteristics of an exceptional society

During the conflict with the Otto Empire Venice came very close, as she had during the Carolingian era, to being absorbed into a western world that would have changed her character radically. It was a hard-fought conflict and was followed by violent internal struggles, resulting in the blood-soaked enmity between the Colprini and Morosini parties becoming permanent. The division between the two families had already given Otto II a strong fifth column in the lagoon region; but here the strength of Venetian society showed itself. A situation such as this would have destroyed any but a healthy society; but at the turn of the millennium Venice, under Pietro II Orseolo (991-1008), one of the greatest Doges in the history of Venice, made a brilliant escape from it.

She was not overawed by the major powers around her but treated with them as an equal. Under Pietro's guidance she obtained favourable conditions from both east and west. Constantinople, which was very important to her commercially, accorded her specially favoured status. Once internal peace was restored, factions within Venice became reunited. Her foreign policy scored unprecedented successes, especially with the victory (in 1002-1003) over the Saracens, who were besieging Byzantine Bari. A still greater triumph was the expedition to Dalmatia. It allowed Orseolo, in the year 1000, to assume the title of "Dux Veneticorum et Dalmaticorum": Doge of Venice and Dalmatia. Relations with Byzantium were by now clearly defined as those of an alliance consolidated by centuries of common interest, without the slightest element of subordination. The strength of Orseolian Venice lay above all, however, in that social warp which can still be glimpsed, in spite of the scarcity of evidence.

The feudalised western part of the region was ruled by a small, rigid class – rigid, but at the same time assured of its superiority, and enclosed in inelastic social structures. Society was stratified according to function: there were those who prayed (the clerics), those who fought (or carried every sort of political responsibility) and those who worked (maintaining those who fought and prayed for them by the sweat of their brow). Compared with such rigid models of society, the little world of Venice was as different as could be: much more ductile and fluid. This was true even of her highest aristocracy, those families from which the Doge was chosen. They were happy to seize the opportunities offered by commerce and financial activity and had no fear of thereby sacrificing dignity and decorum. According to the convictions bequeathed to the middle ages by the culture of the classical, Roman world, a really distinguished social role was not compatible with the market or the management of money. According to that way of looking at things, landed property was in the end the one true, dignified form of riches; prodigality rather than investment was the sign of nobility; war and the exercise of power were the only activities that truly and indubitably belonged to the past.

This reasoning was in clear contrast with that of the Venetians, whose aristocrats, even those most deeply rooted in landed property, and including even the Doges, invested capital and risked money in overseas commercial enterprises *in prima persona*, without dreaming of having to hide behind some front man. The middle centuries of the medieval period were a time of remarkable development for Europe, a time which saw a radical transformation of many things including ethical values. Money became a good and riches an indication of a person's quality. But while Europe as a whole was developing this new climate Venice was already living in it. She was undoubtedly ahead of the rest.

Her strength was based, however, not so much on her "modernity" as on the presence of an unusually large middle class and, still more, on the characteristics of her ruling class. Members of the middle class had enough skill in the fields of economy and commercial enterprise to make their political presence felt. They continued to be excluded from the top positions in government, but the uniqueness of the city's geographical position, together with the difficulties it produced, the opportunities it offered and the needs generated by past political decisions, encouraged them to be enterprising and hard-working. They found their fundamental security in the unity of the state.

Pietro II Orseolo was able to depend on them in his work of consolidating the state by bringing it out of the internal conflicts and the struggles between factions which had troubled so large a part of the tenth century. Venice was finally able to express her potential. Deacon Giovanni, the chronicler, celebrated her prosperity; to him the happiness, the riches and the dignity of the times were such that only divine Providence, "even-handed moderator of all things," could trouble them. Venetian well-being, compared with the harshness of life elsewhere, was worrying to Pope Sylvester II. He wrote to the Doge and to the patriarch of Grado expressing his concern about the corrupted ways of a local clerisy too deeply involved in worldly affairs. It was not just a matter of simony and nicolaism: priests and bishops, immersed in profane lucre "like bankers and stockbrokers", were entangled in the widespread evils of women and the traffic in spiritual goods against which the Church was fighting in her work of reform.

Towards a new balance of forces
in the eleventh century

The fact that Venice had managed to show what role she could play did not mean that her problems were over. Otto Orseolo, the son of Pietro II, succeeded to the title of Doge as if by right, thanks to the prestige of his father, but the old internal tensions very soon reappeared and ended by dislodging him. He was deposed by an uprising in 1027, after his administration had been shaken by the rekindling of internal squabbles and actions, including military action, on the part of the patriarch of Aquileia: the Carinthian Poppus, one of the Counts of Treffen. Aquileia's old claims were all the more dangerous in that the patriarch's moves accorded with the intentions of the Empire, which were once again hostile to Venice. This was particularly evident in 1027 when Corrado II the Salic demanded of the Pope that Aquileia's rights over Grado be recognised, once more claiming ecclesiastical jurisdiction in matters strictly political. But yet again the attempt failed; Venice proved able to defend her complete autonomy, even in the ecclesiastical sphere.

The solidity of her political set-up, her understanding of her own limitations and her firm resolution not to give in on points she considered to be vital all continued to favour her (at that time as well as in the future) and so did a clear and cautious realism which led her to face her circumstances with practical good sense, without excessive worries about prestige or ideological consistency. She survived some rough passages unharmed, thanks to a shrewd understanding of her situation; one such moment occurred during the struggle for the investitures which, in the course of the eleventh century and at the beginning of the twelfth, had seen her confront the Pope and the Emperor in open conflict. The crisis was passed quite calmly, without – in their swings from high to low – damaging Venice's relations with the Emperor, despite pressure from the Pope and the reforming zeal of the Grado Church (especially under the patriarchs Domenico Marango and Pietro Badoer). In all such encounters the Venetians developed a remarkable ability to move with caution along the most complicated paths, but naturally this did not by any means eliminate the possibilities of an open clash. Periodically situations arose in which there was no longer room for compromise and it was necessary to put all her cards on the table. This was very evidently the case in the eleventh century, on the appearance of the Normans in the Adriatic. Increasing worries had already diminished the importance of the old ally Byzantium and increased that of the Hungarians and the Croats in Dalmatia, an area vital to Venice. The situation worsened when in 1075 the Dalmatian cities asked Count Amico, the lord of Giovinazzo in Puglia, for help against the Croatians. That the Normans could, with him, encamp on the eastern shore of the Adriatic, favoured moreover by the support of the Pope, aroused alarming visions of the future. They had already consolidated their control of the Puglia coasts; if they now succeeded in controlling the coasts of Albania and Dalmatia, the Adriatic would be under their dominion. Venice would be suffocated, her way to the north blocked.

Things became even more complicated in the 1080s when Robert the Guiscard began to realise his designs on the Balkans with a project which might reach as far as Constantinople. From 1075-6, first under the Doge Domenico Selvo and then under Vitale Falier, a phase of considerable military involvement opened. More than one clash ended badly for the Venetians (especially when they were not fighting at sea), but once more Venice succeeded in holding her own. The pattern was repeated over and over again: even the worst blows did not succeed in quenching the Venetian capacity for recovery, which for a long time somehow held out.

And so it was on this occasion. The Norman action closed in 1085 with the death of Robert the Guiscard. When he died every plan of conquest vanished into thin air, and Venice emerged from these complicated events more fortunate than ever. Not only had she succeeded in preserving a favourable balance of powers in the Adriatic but she had at the same time secured new privileges in the Byzantine east. The vital importance which her anti-Norman intervention had had for the Constantinople Empire had earned her the gold seal given by Alexander I Comneno in 1082. The ample privileges and abundant approval which the Venetians already enjoyed were consolidated, confirming their economic pre-eminence in the imperial territories.

The crusade intrigue and great power status

From time immemorial, relations with the east were of fundamental importance to the Venetian economy and society, but something new was looming on the horizon which in a few years' time would upset the favourable balance of powers they enjoyed. First and foremost there were the crusades. Appeals to free the holy places and to fight against Islam, and all the first stages of preparing the crusades, saw Venice in the position of anxious spectator, and with some reason. The energies of Christian Europe, which was now in process of vigorous renewal, were poured into a policy of great expansion, with the effect of upsetting the existing balance of power. But what interest could Venice have in modifying political arrangements favourable to her, at the risk of smashing everything to pieces? The liberation of the Holy Sepulchre was close to her heart, naturally, but one had to think carefully about it before gambling on the Syrian or Egyptian markets, or indeed the Byzantine.

All the same, prudence deserted her the moment she saw what advantages her dreaded rivals Genoa and Pisa were deriving from early participation in the crusade. At that point she could no longer remain simply an onlooker. The Serenissima's fleet was to be found at Rodi, Mira in Cilicia, Ascalona, Tyre, Haifa, Acre, Sidon, employed for the sake of prestige in a complex eastern contest whose strategy was aimed at the defence of old privileges, the search for new bridgeheads, the frustration of possible competitors' initiatives, all combined with the fervour of a robust and combative Catholic faith.

To understand the difficulties of the changed times one has only to look at the Pisan-Byzantine agreement of 1111, which opened the markets of Constantinople to extremely threatening competitors, dissolving what had been an almost complete monopoly.

In any case, when in 1130 (after nearly fifty years in which the Doges had come from the Falier and Michiel families) Pietro Polani (son-in-law of his predecessor Domenico Michiel) ascended to the Doge's throne, a particularly complicated phase came to an end without interruption to the progress of prosperity. Venice had, by force of arms, affirmed her position as the strongest maritime power in the eastern Mediterranean. She was strong by virtue of a series of bases and strategic points; she was ready to make herself mistress of a colonial type of dominion.

The chief events which would open the way to the memorable undertaking of 1204, were already discernible at the conquest of Constantinople. And, before that, other episodes marked the stages of enormous development: in particular, towards the middle of the twelfth century, Venice's intervention in the Norman-Byzantine war, when she reconquered Corfu. Corfu was strategically vital to Byzantium and this achievement brought new advantages to the Serenissima, which was now regarded as a great and reliable power. Her prestige was at its height in 1177, when the Venetian government suggested that Venice would be the ideal place for an encounter between Federico Barbarossa and Pope Alexander III. The basilica of St Mark offered the setting for that peace accord between Pope and Emperor which was the beginning of the end of the great crisis of the century. The accord laid the foundations of the Peace of Constance with which, before long, the conflict between Barbarossa and the Italian communes would also be in some way resolved.

When Venice was proposed, as extraneous if not superior to the conflicts between the greatest authorities in Western Christendom, she saw her international reputation grow, and she knew how to capitalize that enhancement of her image, with attention to the rites and liturgies calculated to impress the collective imagination and to consolidate her image as a state. From the ceremonies of 1177 the traditional rituals drew new vigour: the "wedding of the sea", at which the sea was given the propitiatory gift of a ring in sign of the bond and the mastery. And, at the magical moment in which the Pope and the Emperor came into the lagoon to search for peace, the insignia of the Doge which indicated royalty were in part gathered together: the sword, the gold ring, the silver trumpets, the eight vessels, the three canopies, and, as formerly, the sceptre, the throne, the crown. They were the attributes, old and new, of a sovereignty by now indisputable but with singular features. Its greatest representative, the Doge, as the power and complexity of the state of which he was the apex gradually grew, saw his real, personal power diminish.

"Comune Veneciarum"

For centuries the Doge had been the fulcrum of every political compromise, but he now became more and more of a symbol, devoid of real powers. It is true that, because of the uniqueness of the position he occupied, he was always capable of making the full weight of his personality felt, for good or ill; but it is equally true that there had always been a tendency, particularly from the eleventh century onwards, to make of him a living image of what was really important: the state. And in the long centuries of development a vital stage occurred during the afore-mentioned government of Pietro Polani, when for the first time (in 1143) there appears alongside the Doge and his judges "a council of wise men", charged with responsibility for "the honour, profit and security of the state". This new organism, this "Council of Sages" to which the people had to swear obedience, signalled the fact that the institutions of government were undergoing profound modifications. These modifications were even more evident in the almost contemporary appearance (from 1144) of the term *"comune"* (city-state).

The way in which Venice took on the new city-state type of social organisation (which was spreading all over Italy at that time) was as usual highly individual; the lagoon society continued to remodel within its own parameters whatever it could assimilate from the *terrafer-*

ma region. One way and another, the new *comune* outlook broke the traditional bipolarity of Doge-and-people. The impersonal functions and sovereignty of the state came thus to be distinguished from the dwindling personal prerogatives of the Doge. And there began a process that was to modify the essential principles, ethical and political, of Venetian society, so that where once it had seen itself as "Venice, the homeland" it now saw itself as "the city-state of the Venetians".

Things developed fast: in 1143 (as we have seen) there is the first record of the "consilium" of the Wise; in 1165 the whole body of the "bona comunis" (the public assets) was removed from the Doge's full control; in 1172 new procedures for the election of the Doge were introduced, reshaped into a system of unparalleled complexity, the aim of which was to preserve the state from being taken over by groups, parties and favoured individuals, but which only succeeded in seeming suspiciously easy to defraud. In 1192 Enrico Dandolo was the first Doge to be constrained to take the *"Promissione"* (coronation oath). And with the Doge's promise (which was added to the oaths sworn by his immediate predecessors) the Doge solemnly committed himself to the undertakings he would have to maintain in relation to the state and the obligations inherent in his office: a practice always followed thereafter until 1789 when the last Doge, Ludovico Manin, took office. (Continuity was a distinctive trait of the politics and social customs of Venice.)

The process of reducing the regal powers of the Doge was in effect already completed by the end of the thirteenth century. (In the middle of that century it was no longer even permissible to refuse the office.) It went hand in hand with the growth of new organs, offices and magistratures and the construction of a stable and relatively efficient bureaucracy.

The twelfth century had seen the Council of the Wise (later called the Great Council) take the place of the ancient and obsolete assembly of the people. It had wide legislative powers, and the less unwieldy Lesser Council shared with the Doge the duties proper to the executive. Alongside them grew numerous other magistratures: the Avogadori (chief law officers) of the *Comune* had the task of defending the rights of the state and the law; the Giustizieri had to control the guilds which were then being formed; the Visdomini of the Lombards, with those of Ternaria and the Sea, watched over commerce and the collection of import duty; the Camerari or Camerlenghi were the state treasurers; they had to disburse state funds and support the Procurator of St. Mark's, which was a sort of treasury; in the first decades of the thirteenth century the Quarantia (or Council of the Forty) came into being. It was at first a consultative body, then court of appeal and head of the judiciary, first bipartite (covering both civil and criminal law) and then tripartite (when the sector of civil law was divided into two branches). Of the major organs of state with legislative functions the last to appear was the Council of the *Rogati* (or *Pregadi*), later renamed the Senate. Its political and administrative importance grew, from the end of the thirteenth century, until it took the place of the Quarantia.

Other offices, courts and magistratures completed the strong bureaucratic-institutional apparatus which superintended the economic, political and juridical situation of Venice, the lagoons and the overseas territories. Her bureaucracy and her institutions made a solid framework which the Serenissima would on many occasions look to for strength.

The established city

All these changes were accompanied by equally profound modifications to the social and physical fabric of the city. The city of Rialto, which by now we can call Venice by antonomasia, was accepted as the unquestionable capital of the Doge's territory. From 1084 onwards she had reorganised herself on a parochial basis into wards called "confinia" (similar to the *contrade* of other Italian cities) which, under the leadership of *"capi"* (heads), represented the basic units for participation in military, civil and financial functions. Gathered first (towards the middle of the twelfth century) into "*trentacie*" (thirties), the "confinia" were regrouped in about 1175 into six "*sestieri*" (sixths), which survive to this day: Castello, Cannaregio, Dorsoduro, Santa Croce, San Marco and San Polo. The political and administrative organization of the city was based on them; for example the Lesser Council contained one representative from each.

The very fabric of the city was changing, first and foremost in her most prestigious buildings, beginning with the Ducal Palace. It had never before been moved from the property of the Particiaco family, where in 810-811 the Doge Agnello Particiaco had built it. In 976 it had been destroyed by fire in the revolt that dethroned Pietro IV Candiano. It was quickly rebuilt and again ruined by the fire which in 1106 burnt twenty-three parishes. (Fire was a terrifying threat to medieval cities, built of wood and straw.) After that second fire it was immediately restored by Ordelaffo Falier, but in the time of Sebastiano Ziani (1172-1178) a rebuilding was begun that was designed to fit the palace for the new situations obtaining in the city: it was to be a palace (or rather, a complex built in two units) intended for public functions rather than a castle built for defensive purposes. Not for nothing had the times changed.

The work on the Ducal Palace was consistent with the work that was at the same time being done on the *piazza* (the only *piazza*, among many big and small in the city still so called). There were two areas of reconstruction: one was in front of St. Mark's basilica, the other (the *piazzetta*) between the western side of the palace and the *campanile* (bell tower). About a century later the chronicler Martino da Canal was to call it "indisputably the most beautiful *piazza* in the world", and upon it grew the splendour of the basilica, which the chronicler inevitably declared to be "the most beautiful church in the world". Since 829 the basilica had been the centre of the spiritual life of Venice. The Doge Domenico Contarini put its refoundation in hand between 1060 and 1063, modelling it on oriental prototypes, and from then on the process of adorning first the interior and then the façade with precious marble, mosaics and embellishments of every kind continued.

Growth was not limited to the central, most representative areas but affected the entire city. In the first half of the thirteenth century the wooden bridge that was built over the Grand Canal at Rialto assumed a strong symbolic significance, uniting the city's political centre (or "civitas"), seat of civil and religious authority, with the market area. The Arsenal (shipyard), which had started production in the twelfth century, grew rapidly with the growth of the rest of the city and her maritime power, until it became the enormous state shipyard that so appalled Dante. He saw it as one of the circles of hell. It was the biggest unit of productive industry known to the middle ages.

All these new developments entailed the emergence of new families, enriched by commerce, who brought fresh energy to the old ruling class. They produced Doges like Sebastiano Ziani (whose riches were legendary) and his successor Orio Mastropiero (1178-1192). This brings us to the eve of the most astonishing Venetian enterprise of the middle ages: the conquest of an empire and the capture of Constantinople in the fourth crusade.

The fourth crusade. "Dominators of the fourth part and half the Empire"

In Byzantium intolerance of the Latins, and in particular the Venetians, had increased as their power and influence grew. This was demonstrated in 1171 with the Emperor Manuele Comneno's decree that the Venetians should be arrested and their goods confiscated and, worse, in 1182 with the massacre of the Latins in Constantinople. Venetian anxieties about these troubles came to mingle with financial difficulties connected with sending a fourth crusade to the Holy Land. It was delayed in the summer of 1202 by the impossibility of gathering together the great sum agreed with Venice for transport.

A new agreement was reached, which modified the terms of payment in exchange for concrete help. The Doge Enrico Dandolo, blind and very old but still full of extraordinary intuition and ability, transported the crusaders to reconquer Zara which, with the support of the kingdom of Hungary (a traditional adversary), had freed itself from bondage to Venice. Meanwhile the crusading forces decided to make a diversion to Constantinople, summoned by news of dynastic conflicts and requests for help. In the April of 1204 the capital was the scene of destruction and slaughter and fell into the hands of the troops arriving from the west. Christians shed Christian blood – a strange outcome for a crusade.

The Latin Empire of the east came into being under the leadership of Venice. The Doges assumed the title of "dominators of the fourth part and half the Empire" and, when conquered territory was carved up, made it her principle business to acquire bridgeheads and areas that were useful for the control of the seas and commercial routes. Constantinople, Crete, Negroponte in the Aegean, Modone and Corone in the Ionian, together with Adriatic bases and those in the crusader territories functioned as key co-ordination points in the administration of a vast colonial Empire. And if the booty of 1204 brought Venice precious metals and relics, or marble, enamel and goldwork which were then re-used for the gold Pala, and the four bronze horses taken from the Hippodrome of Constantinople to adorn the façade of St. Mark's, the new order of things, for years to come, nourished the flow of goods, business and capital that spread from Rialto all over Europe.

The end of the thirteenth century: new problems and new opportunities

It was a splendid moment for Venice, but her strength inevitably provoked a desire for revenge on the part of Greeks and Byzantines, and the hostility of the competing major powers, starting with Genoa (traditionally her enemy, and previously defeated at St John of Acre in 1258).

The Greek-Genoese alliance, sealed in the treaty of Ninfeo, made the situation dangerous, and the consequent collapse of the Eastern Latin Empire in 1261 made the whole economic and political system of Venice shake perilously, without however producing any decisive damage. The decade 1261-1271, indeed, in spite of being difficult, restored peace and prosperity. It was now very important for Venice that she held dominion over Crete, where (in the absence of Genoese and Greek support) all local resistance was extinguished. This made Venetian control of the Adriatic secure under the vigilant eye of the "Gulf fleet", which combined the functions of policing and military defence.

Only in the last decade of the thirteenth century were really difficult moments to return, with the resumption of war with Genoa for the control of oriental commerce. Venetian ships were beaten by the Genoese at Laiazzo and Curzola in 1294 and 1298, but Genoa did not succeed in making the most of her victories, with the result that Venice came out of the conflict (in the Peace of Milan, 1299) in a fairly favourable situation. The struggle with the Genoese remained unresolved, however, while a deterioration in internal political relations in the course of the last decades of the century coincided with an increase in the sharpness of international competition. This gave added importance to the search for new commercial opportunities and explains Venice's new interest in the west.

Before the end of the thirteenth century the Venetian sailors had sailed into the Atlantic, albeit with privately armed ships and not with convoys or *"mude"* (of which more later) provided by the state. In 1311 they organised the first regular line of navigation towards the North Sea, touching Bruges and London on routes which, however, their Genoese rivals had been using for about forty years. In 1319 five Venetian galleys docked in the port of Southampton. But they continued to search for new possibilities in traditional, eastern directions too. The Polo brothers (as we shall see later) pushed further and further east, and in the course of many years, from 1295, reached beyond the table-land of Pamir and the Gobi desert as far as China, in the Empire of Cathay, in the voyages described by Marco in *Million*.

All these problems and new possibilities, both political and economic, produced tensions and clashes in Venetian society which inevitably ended by being reflected in the city's institutions. The most obvious outcome of such a process came almost at the end of the fourteenth century with the Great Council's "lock-out".

The Great Council's "lock-out" and the beginning of the aristocratic republic

In the last decades of the thirteenth century in Venice a political revolution got underway which was intended to place power exclusively in the hands of a group of families, albeit a large group. Many city-states in Italy, Florence for example, were going through terrible struggles that made the Venetians anxious. After several failed attempts, a law was finally passed, in 1297, that for the first time imposed a narrow limit on accessions to the Great Council. It was the beginning of that political operation which was to be remembered as the "Great Council's lock-out".

Admission to the Council was made steadily more and more difficult for those who had no family connection with it and, finally, in the 1320s, the accession of new men was completely precluded. From that moment, the masculine descendants of those families who were approved during the "lock-out" years had the right to become life members of the Council (from the age of twenty-five or, in certain cases, even earlier). The sovereign body of Venice had become hereditary, and political power had become a prerogative of that body, to the exclusion of everybody else.

The families which, with the *"serrata"*, had assumed exclusive power identified themselves likewise as "patrician" families, as Venetian nobility. It was a rather anomalous nobility, taking its entitlement from its political and administrative functions and for the most part made up of merchants and shipowners, that is, from the upper middle class.

Apart from those sitting in the Great Council from the time of the *"serrata"* (and there were many) some other groups of families were co-opted to the Venetian nobility later in the history of the Republic. Sometimes, as for example after the Chioggia war at the end of the fourteenth century, this was a recognition of merit. At other times it resulted from grave financial need, for example in the Candia war in the second half of the seventeenth century and then again in the second half of the eighteenth.

In the course of the "lock-out" operation there was some resistance. There were one or two attempts to overturn the leading group, captained by the Doge Piero Gradenigo, by force. In 1300 a rich man of the people called Marino Bocconio tried to, with a conspiracy which was repressed without difficulty, and took many with him to the gallows. About ten years later a handful of notables tried, some of whom sat in the Great Council. They formed a conspiracy captained by Baiamonte Tiepolo, Marco Querini and Badoero Badoer. This was in 1310 and their attempted *coup d'état* was played out against the background of a clash with the Pope for control of Ferrara. The conspirators organised themselves well. On the 14th June 1310 (the chronicles of the time are very vivid) a column of armed men marched from the Querini house on Rialto towards San Marco, towards the *piazza* and the Ducal Palace, the very centre of government. In the *piazza* they were supposed to meet another column, of men recruited in the Paduan region, transported across the lagoon by boat. Baiamonte Tiepolo and Marco Querini led the first column, Badoero Badoer the second. During the night, however, the government had heard confused rumours of what was being plotted and the Doge Gradenigo lost no time. He rounded up the Lesser Council, the Heads of the Forty, the *Avogadori di Comun* and whoever else he could, and sent to Chioggia, Torcello, Murano and the Arsenal for help. A tremendous storm was raging. Before reaching the *piazza*, Marco Querini and Baiamonte Tiepolo had divided their columns into two ranks in order to enter it from two directions and both were intercepted. Badoero Badoer and his boats had been caught in the lagoon by the storm and did not arrive at the agreed time. The plot had failed. With Querini killed in battle and Badoer captured, tortured and condemned to death, only Baiamonte Tiepolo succeeded in reaching the Rialto bridge over the Grand Canal, crossing it, breaching it behind him and getting himself and his men safe home behind locked doors on the other side of the canal. There he resisted for as long as he could negotiate, for himself and for those with him, a sort of amnesty which would allow them to leave Venice with only four years' exile in Slavonia as a penalty.

This violent proclamation of opposition to the Doge and the majority who governed the city has been interpreted by some historians as being aimed at thwarting the *"serrata"* and saving the communal nature of the state, but in actual fact not all the motives of the conspiracy are yet clear.

A month after the conspirators were dispersed, the Great Council set up a special and extraordinary tribunal to judge every question connected with the Querini-Tiepolo rebellion. It was supposed to function for only a few months, but its authority was reconfirmed many times until, from 1335 onwards, it became a permanent court. It was the Council of Ten, destined to play a great part in the future government of the Republic.

There were ten members, plus the Doge and the six councillors of the Lesser Council (the heads of the *Quarantia* were included at first, but only until the beginning of the fifteenth century) plus at least one of the *Avogadori di Comun*. (The *Avogadori*, although they had no vote, had a role in all the great political institutions. Their task was to see that the law was kept and they had the power to propose motions that would impede acts they did not consider legitimate).

The Council of Ten showed its mettle almost at once. In 1355 a conspiracy hatched by the Doge himself, Marino Falier, was uncovered. The Ten acted with exemplary speed: within very few days they had arrested the Doge, judged him, condemned him to death and had him beheaded at the doors of the Ducal Palace, where he had sworn his oath of office as Doge. Among all the portraits of the Doges of Venice, which hung in due order in the Ducal Palace, his was covered with a black flag bearing the words "Hic est locus Marini Faletri decapitati pro criminibus" (this is the place where Marini Falier was beheaded for his crimes). Falier's attempt to change the situation had been a strange and clumsy one, intended perhaps to recover all the power that had been lost and vest it in a sort of Lord Doge. (In the rest of Italy this was a time of transition from the city-state type of constitution to the *signoria* type.) However that may be, the disturbing truth that the ruler of the city was also a traitor was made all the more mystifying by a story that was spread about, according to which his motive for leading the conspiracy had been the revelation of his wife's infidelity. It was said to have been made to the Doge by young patricians of rival families, in a note reading (in Venetian dialect): "Marin Falier with the beautiful wife / Others enjoy her and he keeps her". A most improbable infidelity in view of (for one thing) the advanced age of the Doge's wife, Aluica Mocenigo.

As time went on, the Council of Ten extended its functions of supervision, control and political administration to key sectors in the workings of the state: foreign policy, government of the provinces, war and peace, finance, etc., often invading the sphere of other important government departments such as the *Signoria* (the executive) and the Senate and so giving rise to conflicts which led to moments of tense political debate throughout the future history of the Republic. On the other hand, the growing strength of the Council resulted partly from the fact that it was more efficient than the other important committees. It was, in reality, a relatively small institution, free from cumbersome procedures; it had wide powers of discretion and was able to make decisions at the top and keep its operations secret.

A hundred years of war with Genoa for the hegemony of trade with the Levant

With the foundation of the new, aristocratic order of things, the Republic, throughout the fourteenth century, had to undertake complex measures for conquering a prominent place in the control of maritime and commercial traffic in the Levant.

The eastern Mediterranean had undergone considerable change: the states created by the crusades after 1204 had for the most part collapsed; the Latin Empire itself had come to an end in 1261 with the restoration of a Greek Empire which harked back to the Byzantine tradition (the dynasty of the Paleolog family). From the second half of the thirteenth century to the end of the fourteenth, Genoa and Venice, though at long intervals, fought their "hundred years' war", as Gioacchino Volpe put it. The objective of both of them was to gain as complete control as possible of the rich trade with the East, in the most favourable market conditions. The most important moments of the war came at the end of the thirteenth century with the defeat of Venice at Curzola, in the middle of the fourteenth with another Venetian defeat at the Island of Sapienza, and finally in the 1380s with the so-called "war of Chioggia". This began in 1378 and its immediate cause was competition for possession of the island of Tenedo (in the Dardanelles), a centre of Venetian and Genoese traffic and an important base in dealings with Tana and Trebizond, which were staging posts on caravan routes across the Asiatic interior. The Genoese carried the war into the Adriatic, into the very gulf of Venice. Their strategy was based on the fact that the Venetians had plenty on their hands with the Hungarians on account of Dalmatia and the Patriarch of Aquileia on account of Istria, and were moreover under pressure from the Padua *signoria* of the Da Carraras, which aspired to a maritime outlet. There was a moment of acute danger in 1379, when the Genoese took possession of Chioggia and besieged Venice herself. On this occasion the Venetian state institutions showed remarkable firmness: within a few months (thanks especially to the ability of commanders such as Vettor Pisani and Carlo Zen) the situation was reversed and the Genoese, encircled at Chioggia, were forced to surrender. A general peace resulted in 1381 (the Peace of Turin) which, even though it bore heavily on Venice, nevertheless allowed her to lay the foundations of her early fifteenth century expansion. For Genoa, on the other hand, these years saw the beginning of a long decline.

Commerce

There were important developments in the Venetian maritime and commercial economy in the fourteenth and fifteenth centuries.

Together with a general growth in the exchange of goods at European level, Venice established herself as one of the best equipped markets for exchange between Europe and the Mediterranean coasts. Textiles, metals, furs, worked amber, and various manufactures from the west passed through Venice on their way to the Mediterranean. Spices, cotton, incense and perfumes, silk, alum, dyes and sugar arrived in Venice from the shores of the eastern Mediterranean destined for Europe, and some of these products had come by land from China, India, south-east Asia, and the interior of Africa. From the Slav countries came honey, wax and furs, to be exchanged for salt, textiles and metal alloys.

As Venice gradually gained control of the Adriatic, she began to build up a number of legal, financial and military measures, all of them directed towards establishing the Venetian port as the nerve-centre of maritime and commercial operations economically important not only for the operators' profits but also for the state's finances. These measures included, for example, some which made it obligatory for Venetian merchants to have their merchandise carried only by Venetian ships; others which made it obligatory for Venetian ships to carry the merchandise of foreign merchants only on condition that they passed through Venice; others which made it obligatory for merchant ships crossing the Adriatic to call at Venice; and still others which prohibited the building of ships for foreigners. All this gave the city a greater and greater share in the control and management of maritime trade. It also meant the exaction of harbour dues, the encouragement of the shipbuilding industry and related armature, and the development of service industries and highly skilled manufacture of various kinds. To sum up, there were not only boundless opportunities for the very remunerative investment of capital but also growth, at times almost by geometrical progression, of the accumulation and redeployment of capital. There were also enormous returns for the state (not least from harbour dues); increased riches for classes and individuals; a flourishing labour market; fairly general approval of the political and economic authorities; and growth in urban organization, characterised to some extent by the requirements of the city's principal interests, which were commerce and shipping. And all this, naturally, without discouraging the foreign operators, who gradually gave up using land routes through Italy and Europe for goods taken to and from Venice. They were further attracted by special conditions introduced with the purpose of making things easier for them; for instance, the Fondaco at Rialto (which began to be built in the first half of the thirteenth century) was given to the German merchants and provided them with warehouses, living quarters, services and various commercial concessions.

The most important areas of the city were San Marco, the seat of government, Castello, the home of the Arsenal, and Rialto, which was the area of the great markets, whose institutions were public property. It was also the financial district and that of the courts concerned with money and with the running of the city; the district of the slaughter-houses (*"beccarie"*), warehouses, depositories, craftsmen's workshops, inns and taverns; and the district where commercial operators of every kind (often foreigners) lived, together with ships' crews on shore leave and men employed in transport and warehouses. It was also, to begin with, the red light district; in the fourteenth and fifteenth centuries there were a number of brothels there which together made up "the little Castello", a part-public part-private business.

As we have said before, the merchants were, and for a long time remained, the most significant component of Venetian society. Their imprint on government was clear. Many of them, down the centuries, became explorers and left records of their adventurous travels. Among the many who became explorers and left records of their adventures one thinks of Marco Polo, whose journeys in the second half of the thirteenth century (recounted in his book *Million*) took him as far as China. Others who come to mind are Nicolò de' Conti from Chioggia, who in the early years of the fifteenth century travelled in south Asia and left an account of it; Cesare Federici, Gasparo Balbi and other sixteenth-century merchant travellers in India. There were merchant navigators, too, from Alvise Da Mosto to the Cabots who, working for the Portuguese, the Spanish and the English, explored the African and American coasts.

In 1284 a gold coin called the ducat (3.5 grams, 24 carat) began to be minted. It was later called the *zecchino* and was destined to become at least as prestigious in Europe and the Mediterranean as the Florentine florin. Alongside the gold currency there was the silver and many kinds of copper coins. The Zecca was the famous state mint.

The most important factors competing for the organisation of Venetian commercial and maritime enterprise were investment capital, the industry and management of ships and state intervention.

It is worth considering some of the practices by which Venetian enterprise was made profitable. For example, a venture could be financed by a maritime loan with a fairly high annual rate of interest; or, under the terms of a partnership contract, a financier, a merchant or a merchant-shipowner formed a partnership and the merchant went off to use the capital entrusted to him abroad; on his return the capital was repaid and the profits, less expenses, were divided between the partners in proportion to their investment. From the fourteenth century commercial companies known as *"fraterne"* were also quite common. This kind of company was a sort of society of partners with a collective name, and was usually a family affair. The partners pooled their capital and their work and shared responsibility for the undertakings that each made; profit and loss were shared among them according to the proportion of their investment.

In the late medieval period, operations of exchange, movement of money and credit were refined. The techniques of the current account and the double entry system of accounting began very early in Venice. Merchants could pay each other simply by presenting a document. Operations like this could be made through banks called *"banchi di scripta"* or "clearing banks". In order to give banking more stability and reassure depositors, a semi-public bank was founded in the second half of the sixteenth century called the *Banco della Piazza di Rialto* and finally, in 1619, a completely public bank was established called the *Banco del Giro*.

In the middle of the fifteenth century the methods of handling public finance too were perfected: alongside the traditional systems of indirect taxation (dues) and obligatory loans levied on citizens, which had created a vast national debt (*Monte Vecchio*, then *Montenuovo* and the *Nuovissimo* of the *Sussidio*), direct taxes were introduced, among them the very substantial *decime* (tithes).

Ships

If the investments and the trading arrangements were important factors in Venetian commerce, the shipbuilding industry and the organization of shipping were equally so. The Venetian navigation in the Mediterranean (and not, therefore, in the lagoons or the rivers) was essentially based on two types of ship: the "round ships" and the "long ships" or galleys. The round ships were like walnut shells in outline, with after-castle and fore-castle, and had one or three masts; they had lateen sails and later, in part at least, square sails. The galleys, on the other hand, were long, narrow and flat-bottomed, with low sides; they were propelled by oars, with the help of sails when necessary. The round ships carried a greater quantity of goods (usually bulky rather than valuable, such as grit, salt and so on) and did not require a big crew. Typical round ships of the thirteenth and fourteenth centuries were the *"cocche"*; later the *"caracche"* were popular and, above all as ships of war, galleons and frigates. The galleys were better at arriving at their destinations punctually, thanks to their oar-power, but they needed very large crews. The most important of them were called "heavy" or "market" galleys (200-300 or more tons of cargo and two hundred men, most of them oarsmen); "narrow galleys", which were more manoeuvrable and used for war; and the formidable but slow *"galeazze"*, warships which were to play an important part as late as 1571, at the battle of Lepanto.

A particular system of navigation, used principally for the shipment of valuable merchandise, was that of convoys; it was a system in which the interest and intervention of the state combined well with the interest and management of private operators. In the fourteenth and fifteenth centuries the system, which had been gradually worked out in preceding eras, was used for a series of Mediterranean and ocean shipping routes: first of all the *"muda"* (regular voyage) to Romania, with Constantinople as the chief port of call, the Syrian *"muda"* calling at Cyprus, Beirut and Laiazzo, and the Alexandrian *"muda"* to Egypt; thereafter the Flanders *"muda"*, with calls in England and the Flanders; the Aigues-Mortes *"muda"* (near Marseilles) with Tyrrhenian, French and Spanish calls; the Barbery *"muda"*, with Tripoli, Tunis, etc. as ports of call; and finally the *"tràfego"* line, consisting of Venetian ships plying to and for between various north African ports.

Besides constituting a regular service, convoys guaranteed greater safety from shipwreck, pirate attack and so on, and so lowered the risk-cost (for example, insurance premiums) to merchants. Some of these voyages were annual, others occurred several times a year. There were usually about ten "market galleys" in a convoy, but often fewer.

In the first quarter of the fourteenth century, the Venetian Senate, which is to say the state, took certain aspects of the management of the *"mude"* more directly in hand. They fixed the periods of the year in which voyages were to take place, indicating the routes to be covered, the places and times at which calls were to be made, and specifying what merchandise was to be carried. It was always to be valuable: manufactured goods, precious metals, etc. on the outward voyage; spices, dyes, precious stones, etc. on the return voyage. Above all, the state supplied the ships used on the *"mude"*.

They were built in the Arsenal, which was gradually enlarged until it became the imposing shipyard of the sixteenth century, one of the greatest industrial concentrations in Europe at that time. The Arsenal was, and remained, state-owned. The provision of ships for the voyages was managed by auction (known as "the galley auction"); a ship was rented out to the highest bidder for a single voyage.

Marine insurance was already widespread in the fifteenth century. An "agent", using forms on which were written the data about the ship, the cargo, the voyage and the mount of insurance required, assembled the signatories who wanted to take shares in this piece of insurance business. The premium varied (usually between 2.5 % and 5%) according to the general circumstances and the consequent assessment of the magnitude of risk.

Apart from the big galleys of the *"mude"*, which were built in the Arsenal, many galleys of various kinds and most of the round ships of various types were built in the numerous private shipyards (*"squeri"*) scattered all over the city, and the management of them was also largely private.

The decline of the heavy merchant galleys began in the sixteenth century.

State intervention made a decisive contribution to the success of Venetian maritime commerce. Such intervention was more considerable in Venice than elsewhere (in Genoa, for instance); the management of shipping was governed, as Ferdinand Braudel writes, by the criteria of an *"économie dirigée"* (centrally directed economy). The important thing, as Gaetano Cozzi notes, was to "guarantee that Venetian commerce was present wherever possible and in privileged conditions which gave it subsidies, privileges and the political and organisational support of the state".

When necessary the merchant ships were transformed into battleships. The Arsenal was responsible for fitting, maintaining and repairing them.

Whereas land troops were organised with hired mercenary leaders who had nothing to do with the government of Venice, though under the political control of the army *Provveditori* (Commissioners), the naval forces had a hierarchy of command based on the political personnel of the Republic. In time of peace, this hierarchy was essentially formed by the *Provveditore Generale* of "the sea state" (that is, Venice and the lagoon region), who was usually resident in Corfu, by the *Provveditore Generale* in Dalmatia and Albania (usually based in Zara) who took care of the specific combat area, and by the gulf Captain, who commanded the small fleet which Venice kept at sea in time of peace with the task of patrolling the Adriatic to keep an eye on her boasted sovereignty in the gulf itself.

In time of war the chain of command was formed by the Captain general of "the sea state", who was not so much an expert on military operations as an administrator who needed the gifts of an organiser, a diplomat and a politician rolled into one. He was assisted by the *Provveditore all'armata* (Commissioner for the armed forces) and by other officers whom he summoned, when circumstances required it, for a consultation (often enlarged by the addition of further advisors) to make important decisions.

Various ways were tried to solve the problem of recruiting sailors, oarsmen and even soldiers. Alongside the volunteers, conscripts were enrolled in Candia, in Dalmatia and in the other Venetian territories. In about 1545 it was decided that galleys should be manned by those condemned to serve in them as a punishment, a sentence which the criminal courts began to inflict with alacrity.

The fifteenth century, the "land state"

Until the fourteenth century Venice's interests had lain principally in the Mediterranean and not in the Italian peninsula, but in the fifteenth she was obliged to become deeply involved in the political situations that were being created in the Venetian hinterland, which lay behind the narrow strip of lagoons constituting the Doge's territory. Some of the *signorie* (governments consisting of overlords) which had taken the place of *comuni* (city-states with a republican style of government) attempted to extend themselves in Veneto, and all but achieved the dimensions of a regional state. The Scaligeri family attempted to do this in Verona in the first half of the fourteenth century and the Da Carraras of Padua in the second half. Their attempts failed, partly owing to the fact that their opponents received armed support from the Venetians, to whom the possibility that their *terraferma* hinterland might be transformed into a regional state was a dire threat. Such a state would be capable of damaging their economy by attaining control of their lines of communication with Italy and Europe and their supply routes from the north. It might even have the military capacity to drive them into the sea.

The Scaligeris' attempt was thwarted by force (the Venetians had the Florentines as their principal allies) and, at the end of the war (in 1339), Venice found herself in control of Treviso and part of the Trevigiano.

The attempts of the Da Carraras after the middle of the fourteenth century were at first checked, in spite of being supported by the Hungarians and the Dukes of Austria. However, they were renewed towards the end of the 1370s in the Chioggian war, which ended with the Peace of Turin in 1381. On that occasion Venice had to resist a swarm of sovereign peoples, each with its own objectives (the Genoese, the Hungarians, the Patriarch of Aquileia, the Da Carraras ...). This second attempt of the Da Carraras was also checked.

At last, at the end of the century, the conclusive match was played. The Da Carraras allied themselves with Giangaleazzo Visconti, the Lord of Milan, and did not realise that their fellow adventurers were too powerful for them. It was the Milanese who took Verona, Vicenza, Feltre and Belluno. At first Venice, cleverly, forebore to show too much opposition, seeking to let the situation play their game against the Da Carraras for them. Then, when Visconti had taken almost all of Veneto and it had become obvious, therefore, that he was a greater danger than the Da Carraras, the Venetians went back to helping Francesco Novello Da Carrara. They did not, however, succeed in improving a situation which was becoming critical. What turned matters in Venice's favour was the death, in 1402, of Giangaleazzo and the opening of a crisis of succession in Milan. Venice succeeded in taking over Feltre, Belluno, Bassano, Vicenza, Verona, Padua and the territory surrounding them, besides (for a time rather insecurely) part of Polesine. She absorbed them all between 1404 and 1406, adding them to Treviso, which was hers already, and had been since 1339 except for a brief interval. All the new acquisitions were achieved partly by dealing with Giangaleazzo Visconti's widow and partly by imposing "reparations" on them by a mixture of diplomatic skill and force.

The "land state", at the beginning of the fifteenth century, was therefore an accomplished fact; to the territorial components of the "sea state" presided over by the Doge, the Republic of Venice had added the Venetian *terraferma*. Within a short time, after a cycle of wars and truces with the Hungarians (from 1409 to the so-called "war of Friuli" of 1418-1420) she had added part of Friuli including Udine, at the same time stabilising her control over Istria and Dalmatia. These changes were formalised in a series of treaties, from that of Prague in 1437 with the Hungarians to those of 1445 and 1451 with the Patriarchy of Aquiliea.

In the spring of 1423 the Doge Tommaso Mocenigo, feeling that he was close to death, made a speech to his closest government colleagues which has come down to us. In this speech (whether authentic or edited) the Doge outlined a totally positive report on the state of the Republic; on Venice's commercial, maritime and financial strength; on the excellence of her political and administrative institutions; on the durability of the systems on which the "sea state" was based; and on the solidity already achieved in the "land state". According to the aged Doge, the power they had achieved was sufficient. Venice should take care not to seek further territorial expansion in Italy and not to get dragged into disputes between the states of the peninsula; she should take care not to elect Francesco Foscari as Doge, since he was "a hawk" (Tommaso Mocenigo used that very term) who would take Venice into war, to the destruction of her economic resources and the loss of honour and reputation.

After his death, things fell out exactly as

Tommaso Mocenigo had feared: once Francesco Foscari had been elected Doge he continually interfered in the struggles for expansion that had for a long time been going on in Italy. Exhausting wars, one following hard on another, fed by the mirage of conquering the hegemony which confused the aims of some of the regional states: Milan, the Republic of Florence, the Pope, and the Naples first of the Angioi and then of the Aragonese; but principally the Republic of Venice.

In northern Italy the expansionist pressure from the Duke of Milan, Filippo Maria Visconti, had driven the two republics – Florence and Venice – to form an alliance against him in 1425. Fighting broke out and was extinguished several times. In the course of all this, Francesco Bussone, known as *"il Carmagnola"*, a mercenary leader in the employ of Venice, in spite of his victory at Maclodio was suspected of treachery. In 1432, accused by the Council of Ten, he was condemned to death for collusion with the enemy. The court records do not survive and the justice of his conviction is still debated.

In the course of all this fighting, Venice added to her "land state" the Lombard provinces of Bergamo, Brescia and Crema.

Between 1435 and 1454 there was endless fighting and an endless succession of alliances, endlessly made, turned on their heads, and broken. When Philippo Maria died in 1447, and was replaced by the Golden Ambrosian Republic of Milan, Venice shilly-shallied, so that the Milanese ended by attaching themselves to Francesco Sforza. He was one of those mercenaries who were emerging to fill the spaces that no Italian state managed to occupy entirely, either by force or by hegemonic state programmes.

The extremely confused cycle of wars closed with the Peace of Lodi in 1454. The Venetians reached an agreement with Sforza, Italy's new strong man.

Once the construction of the "land state" had been completed by the acquisition of Bergamo, Brescia and Crema, the rulers of Venice might perhaps have thought about a sort of "refoundation" of the state, which reckoned realistically with the territorial and human components of the Republic. That did not happen. Even in the "land state" all that was done was to establish bilateral relations between the dominant city (Venice) and each of the subject territories, on the basis of those acts of submission and reparation included in the truce pacts during the recent fighting. The subject territories were allowed to keep their autonomy in their constitutions and in the local institutions of administration, but it was an autonomy which was gradually eroded, and meanwhile every important political and economic decision had to be submitted to Venice. The people who dealt with these subject territories, even in the "land state", were those figures of rather ambiguous institutional aspect known as Rectors (or, elsewhere, as *podestà*, *camerlengo*, Captain, etc.) They were appointed by Venice, in rather rapid succession. The Rectors were not so much governors as political mediators between Venice and the subject territories. They also had to mediate between the cities and the country surrounding them, and between those involved in local quarrels. The Rectors were often intent on reaping advantage for Venice from such tensions, but above all they were intent on not letting them get more acute, not letting them explode.

The Turks

In the middle of the fifteenth century Europe and the Venetians were presented with a new player in the war game: the Ottoman Empire.

The Osman Turks who constituted the original nucleus of the Empire belonged to a Turcoman tribe who came down – in the second half of the thirteenth century – from the table-lands of Armenia and settled in Anatolia. Under the leadership of Othman I (from whom comes the name of 'Ottoman') they had obtained territorial control in Asia Minor on their way to Europe. Mahomet II, "the conqueror" (1451-1481), having at his disposal a well-organized, numerous, and in some ways modern army, a war fleet recently built and fitted, a huge reserve of men and material and a state organization in process of construction along strong and original lines, with a unitarian religion and ideology like Islam, realised extremely ambitious designs of conquest. In 1453 he devastated Constantinople, putting an end for ever to the last vestige of the Eastern Roman Empire and transforming the great city into a political, economic and social centre of the areas which were one after the other to become the victims of rapid and extensive Turkish conquest.

The Venetians had received warning of the potential danger in 1429-30, when Salonica, which had been ceded to her in 1423, was snatched from her by the Ottoman armies (Earlier Turkish attacks had been repulsed quite easily.). But the real alarm came in 1453 with the fall of Constantinople.

The siege of Constantinople lasted about two months. The Venetian sailors and merchants belonging to a little fleet of galleys which happened to be in the port were involved, and Nicolò Barbaro, a ship's doctor, has left us in his *Journal of the Siege of Constantinople* a testimony to their sense of civic responsibility in the meetings at which they decided what to do with the ships and cargoes entrusted to them and with their own lives and goods. Giuliano Lucchetta has described Barbaro's Journal thus: the narration is lucid and concrete and nothing, or very little, is conceded to emotion, even when he describes in detail and with extraordinary effect the horror of the slaughter and sacking that went on while bells sounded and the population knelt in the churches and the squares weeping and praying. Janissaries sprang out of the smoke of the mortars, to the sound of the kettle drums, "like lions skinning the earth and whatever they found on the earth. Everyone fell to the scimitar of the Turk, women as well as men, the old and babies too, people of every condition. The slaughter lasted from dawn ... to mid-day ... ; blood ran over the earth like rain, in rivulets; the dead bodies, Turk and Christian, were thrown into the Dardanel, which carried them down to the sea as melons are carried down the canals".

After the Venetians in 1454 had arrived at a peace with the Turks and had obtained recognition of their colony at Constantinople ·(the Venetian *bailo* (consul) was to become to all intents and purposes ambassador to the Sultan), Mahomet continued his policy of expansion, penetrating Greece and Serbia. The Hungarians and Venetians, encouraged by Pius II, set on foot an anti-Turk crusade, partly to give support to the resistance of Scandenberg (Giorgio Castriota) in Albania. The war dragged on from 1463 to 1479; Mahomet reached a point near Belgrade; bands of Turkish raiders got as far as the borders of Friuli in Veneto; and in 1470 Venice lost the important base of Negroponte. Under the terms of the peace agreement that ended the conflict Venice was obliged to recognise the Turkish presence in Albania and the Aegean and to pay tribute periodically in money to the Sublime Port. In 1480 the Turks, setting sail from Valona, disembarked on the coast of Puglia and conquered and sacked Otranto, but the death of Mahomet II the following year led to their losing Otranto and getting thrown out of Italy.

The Venetians were in a way compensated for the losses suffered in the Aegean by the acquisition of the important island of Cyprus. It was a long job: in the sixties they succeeded in making Catherine Cornaro marry the King of the island, Giacomo di Lusignano (the Lusignano dynasty went back to the time of the crusades); in 1473, making the most of the fact that she had been widowed, they surrounded her ·with counsellors; finally, in 1488, they induced her to abdicate in favour of Venice, giving her as compensation the title of "daughter of the Republic". The island, besides being a strategic base of great significance on the routes between the West and Syria, produced abundance of sugar, salt and wine.

All the same, shortly afterwards, between 1499 and 1503, the Venetians lost a new war. The naval defeat of the Zonchio entailed the loss of the two strategic bases of Modone and Corone at the extreme south of the Morea, that is, the Peloponese.

Crisis in the first decade of the
sixteenth century.
"Reflection"

The formation, well underway at the end of the fifteenth century, of two "national" states like France and Spain began to change the equilibrium of Europe. The two monarchies began to look at Italy as a place where they could demonstrate their power.

Charles VIII of France crossed the Alps in the autumn of 1494. His army took Naples without any difficulty. Astonishment at the ease of his conquest was followed by the formation of an anti-French league (in Venice in 1495) whose armies fought the "ultramontanes" at Fornovo near Parma. The outcome of the battle was not clear, and Charles was able to return to France. When he died in 1498 he still intended to invade Italy again. Meanwhile, the kingdom of Naples threw off its French rulers with the help of the Spanish, who had landed in Calabria (Spain having joined the anti-French league of 1495). They were also assisted by the Venetians, who landed in Puglia and occupied various ports such as Gallipoli, Brindisi, Trani and Otranto, which they held for some time.

Charles VIII's sortie into Italy marked the beginning of a period of history that was to be a time of crisis in the Italian states in which the Renaissance was born. The whole peninsula was to become the battleground of several great European powers.

In Granada in 1500 France and Spain agreed to take possession of the kingdom of Naples and divide its territory between them. Venice stood aside, foreseeing that the agreement would not last long. She was right. The two allies fought each other, and Ferdinand the Catholic of Spain won. Peace was made in the treaty of Blois (1504) by which Naples was allotted to Spain and Milan to France. A year before that, Caesar Borgia, the Valentine, son of Pope Alexander VI, had planned to create a state between Marches and Romagna for himself, but his plan had failed. Venice at once took advantage of the failure and, by means of the usual "reparations" (ceded cities) took possession of Faenza, Rimini, Fano and various other cities which were strategically important and which were claimed by Julius II, the successor of Alexander VI and Pius III.

Questions relating to Venice and all that was going on in Italy came to the ears of Maximilian of Hapsburg. For a long time he tried to reach an anti-French understanding with Venice, but in vain. Then in 1507 he wanted to march down to Rome to have himself crowned there, but this entailed crossing Venetian soil and Venice refused permission. He decided to resort to war, but was repeatedly defeated and in the end, under an armistice of 1508, had to hand over Gorizia, Trieste and Fiume to Venice.

It looked as if fortune would continue to smile on the Republic, but in fact a formidable coalition was being quickly formed against her. France and the Empire first (at the Peace of Cambrai, 1508) and then Spain, agreed to settle their differences in various parts of Europe and Italy, partly by means of reciprocal compensation which would be made possible by the dismemberment of the Venetian state. A little later these three powers were joined by Pope Julius II and various Italian princelings.

In the early months of 1509 the French started hostilities along the Adda, Maximilian descended on Veneto to the north, the Spaniards reconquered the Puglian ports, and Julius II excommunicated Venice. On the 14th March of that year the Venetian army was defeated by the French at Agnadello near Ghiara d'Adda. Everything seemed to crumble rapidly: the Republican troops were dispersed; Bergamo, Brescia and other cities got rid of their Venetian Rectors; Padua fell into enemy hands and then, after being recaptured, was besieged by Imperial troops.

Many factors combined to save the situation, among them the realism and pragmatism of the political and diplomatic action taken by the Venetian leaders, with the object of sowing dissension among the allies, all of whom were pursuing their own interests. Recovery was also helped by organisational and financial skill and by the staying power of the Venetian political and administrative institutions, which helped to preserve the vitally important loyalty of the common people and, especially, the peasants.

Almost at once, Julius II, placated by Venice with the restitution of the cities of Romagna and Marche, realised the danger of a French preponderance and set to work to undo the alliance. The result was the "Holy League" (1511) of Rome, Spain and Venice against France, and the battle of Ravenna. The battle was won by the French but they nevertheless had to return to France.

Wars and alliances continued to pile up tumultuously in Europe and in Italy. The Venetians made friends with the French again and gave them assistance in the "Battle of the Giants" at Marignano in 1515, which they won against the armies of the Emperor, the Pope and Spain. Between 1516 and 1519 Ferdinand the Catholic of Spain and the Emperor Maximilian of Hapsburg died, and this resulted in the unification of an immense amount of Spanish and Imperial territory, as both of them were succeeded by their grandson, Charles of Hapsburg. He took the title of Charles V and his dominions extended from Spain to north Italy, Germany, Flanders and the Danubian possessions of the Hapsburgs, to say nothing of territory acquired by discovery and conquest in America.

At this point Venice felt threatened by such a huge increase in Hapsburg power and re-established a bond with France. It lasted until 1523, when it seemed a good idea to draw nearer to Charles V, who defeated Francois I of France in 1525 at the battle of Pavia, took him prisoner and compelled him to accept the terms of the Peace of Madrid. In the next few years Charles V – although heavily engaged with the Turks and with the Protestant Reformation which had by now taken root in many of the Imperial territories – took Italian affairs in hand once more (the sack of Rome, 1527) and, when the fresh conflict with Francois I was over, negotiated the re-organization of the peninsula at the Congress of Bologna (1529-30) with Pope Clement VII. The Congress formalised on an international plane the re-acquisition by Venice of her "land state" (that is, Veneto, apart from Friuli, Bergamo, Brescia and Crema).

The rulers of Venice were gradually becoming conscious that the Republic's power had diminished. Between 1537 and 1540 they found themselves at war with the Turk once more. They had Charles V and the Pope on their side, but it was an involvement in war which they had made every effort to avoid. After a defeat at sea, suffered at Prevesa in the Ionian, they made a separate peace which, at the cost of territorial sacrifices (the loss of, among other places, Naples, Romania and Malvasia), preserved their Levant trade. Suliman II, "The Magnificent", had extended the Ottoman Empire vastly, to include even the Mediterranean coasts of Africa and the Danubian plain.

The half-century that had seen far-reaching changes in Europe and Italy, the establishment of the Protestant Reformation and, after decades of geographical discovery, the beginnings of enormous colonial exploitation overseas, can be considered to close with the death of François I of France, with the abdication of Charles V (who divided the Hapsburg dominions between his brother Ferdinand I and his son Philip II) and with the Peace of Cateau-Cambrèsis (1559) which carved Italy up in a way that was destined to last for some time (Spain remained installed in Lombardy, in the Kingdom of Naples, in Sicily and in Sardinia).

For the first decades of the sixteenth century the rulers of Venice were stunned by a sort of terrified amazement. They had to realise that all around them, in Italy and in Europe, worlds were changing; they had to take in the newness of the strategies and conceptions of power of such states as had embarked on "modernity" and now considered expansion, centralisation, strategic influence and the economic exploitation of huge continental and extra-continental areas absolutely vital. Of these states, France and Spain were the most important. As time went by, that terrified amazement became a memory; the startling evidence and immediacy of all this newness faded; and somehow, in the general crisis of Italian freedom, the independence of the Venetian state had been saved. At that point Venice was capable of understanding the limits within which she would have to live and the limits of any possible relationship with the new kind of European state.

"Reflection" and "detachment" were among the one-word formulas which attempted to express the fundamental lines of a new policy (which was, in a nutshell, neutrality towards European wars and conservatism with regard to Venetian institutions and society). This was the policy which the rulers of Venice thought out and put into practice from the middle of the sixteenth century; these were the political lines which were destined, however much they were diluted, suspended or contradicted, to last through the centuries to come.

Venice the great city

Judged simply by her dimensions and the variety of her activities, the Venice of the first half of the sixteenth century was a great metropolis. Her size and prosperity had reached their peak at the end of the preceding century. Thereafter, her overseas trade continued on a great scale, though at some cost to investment in land and in ships (a change that was contested).

People came to the city from everywhere, and immigration from Venice's dominions on land and sea continued to be massive; there were busy communities of Greeks, Albanians, Armenians, Germans and Jews (the Ghetto began in 1516). Venice was a great melting-pot which felt all the uncertainties and anxieties of the time as an experience of her own at this culminating moment in her history. An image of this fervid, fascinating city remains to us in various records, notably the monumental *Diaries* (covering the years 1496-1533 in 58 volumes) of the great chronicler Marino Sanudo, and in the admirable and extremely detailed bird's eye view printed by Jacopo de' Barbari (1500).

In the first centuries of her existence Venice had been built almost entirely of wood and was therefore often a prey to fire; but from the thirteenth century she was gradually transformed into a city of stone. In those early days it had been necessary to improve the ground and elevate it in order to be able to lay foundations on it, but later it became the rule to drive a dense network of poles (as much as ten metres long) into the soft lagoon soil on which to build foundations. Venice rests on millions of trees stuck head down in mud. Houses and palaces, public and private (the Ducal Palace being the first) were built and rebuilt over the centuries, together with churches, monasteries and bell towers (scores and scores of them, from the basilica of St Mark to the monasteries of the Franciscans and the Dominicans, who were among the first religious orders to establish themselves in the city). The shape and direction of the canals were changed (the Canal Grande was an exception), dozens of bridges were thrown over them, a road system was built, accessibility by water was organized, suitable boats invented (the gondola being the most notable). Defence works were constructed to protect the lagoon from the sea and from the rivers. One architectural style after another left traces which blended with the next style: Gothic, Roman and Byzantine stood side by side. The city of the fourteenth century was Gothic, albeit with hints at independence (ornate Gothic) and with some touches of Byzantine revival. Finally Venice too set out on the road to humanism and the classical Renaissance, which would be established by the sixteenth century. Great names begin to emerge, and that means, in architecture and sculpture, Antonio Rizzo and the Lombards and Mauro Codussi, and then Sansovino, and Andrea Palladio, and Michele Sanmicheli ... , and, in painting it means Andrea Mantegna and the Bellinis, and Carpaccio, and Giorgione, and then Titian, Lotto, Palma the Old, Sebastiano del Piombo, Tintoretto, Paolo Veronese ..., and, in every sector of culture, including the sciences, it means achievements of great interest. The political and social character of the Republic, crystallised gradually in the period of "reflection", could no long be reformed; it began, on the contrary, to be part of the paraphernalia of the so-called "myth of Venice". But Andrea Gritti – a great Doge of the first half of the sixteenth century – at least set moving a "renovatio urbis" (renewal of the city), a reform of the urban image of the places that give the city its individuality.

The population grew enormously: there were about 130,000 in the fourteenth century, more than 150,000 in the fifteenth and sixteenth. Manufactures grew enormously, too, and the work of skilled craftsmen, even those not connected with shipbuilding: textile products (wool, silk, cotton, linen ...); "chemical" products (dyes, soap, saltpetre and gunpowder, medicines such as the famous cure-all *"teriaca"*; glass (Murano); building materials; sugar refining; goldwork and jewellery; work in coral, amber, leather (gilded leatherwork especially), skins ... Typography and publishing reached remarkable heights. (If we mention only one among the artists in this field, that one must be Aldo Manuzio.)

There was also a great increase in the guilds of those working in manufacture, crafts and services. There were more than a hundred in the sixteenth century; they contributed greatly not only to the protection of their members but also to the solidarity of Venetian society and the maintenance of the consensus of the populus, a consensus on which the state could always count.

The formation of associations like these played a part in another important sector: social welfare. There were hundreds of fraternities, schools, hospices and hospitals great and small, such as the great schools of S. Maria della Carità, S. Giovanni Evangelista, S. Maria della Misericordia, St. Mark, St. Rocco, S. Teodoro, St. Maria del Carmelo and the great hospices and hospitals like S. Maria della Pietà (the home for waifs and strays), the hospitals for Incurabili (Incurables), Derelitti

(Homeless), Mendicanti (Beggars), Zitelle (Spinsters), Catecumeni (Catechumens), Convertite (Converts), Soccorso (Succour), Penitenti (Penitents), etc. This network of care was created in the middle ages and developed in the sixteenth century, then developed further in the seventeenth and eighteenth. There were thousands and thousands of people who were served by these institutions or who provided them: the whole population of Venice was linked together by them. They were institutions which were inspired by Christian charity but directed by laymen. Their work of developing social solidarity and social welfare was, in the course of centuries, enormous; their headquarters were often decorated with important works of art; their accumulated assets became huge at times (mostly endowments provided by individuals). Through these corporate activities people were able to have a part in the myth of Venice and also in the reality.

Lepanto

At the beginning of 1570 the Turks claimed the island of Cyprus. Shortly afterwards they occupied most of it, with the exception of the stronghold of Famagosta, which put up a splendid resistance to siege. Venice tried up to the last minute to negotiate and avoid war, but then had to prepare to join forces with Pius V and Philip II of Spain to fight the Ottomans.

The Christian fleets were concentrated at Messina in the summer of 1571 (more than two hundred galleys, six war galleys and a certain number of lesser craft; a fleet of which more than half, including the six war galleys, was composed of Venetian ships, while the rest was composed of ships belonging to Spain, the Pope and a few minor nations). The supreme command had been entrusted to Don John of Austria, the natural son of Charles V; Marcantonio Colonna was the papal commander; Gian Andrea Doria commanded the Spanish; Sebastiano Venier and Agostino Barbarigo were the two Venetian commanders. The Turkish fleet, which was concentrated in the gulf of Lepanto, was composed of more than two hundred galleys and a large number of smaller ships, and was commanded by Alì Pascià.

The clash came on 7 October 1571 in the gulf of Lepanto. The two fleets were drawn up opposite each other, each presenting a slightly concave line to the enemy. The Venetian war galleys, towed into a position in front of the Christian fleet, performed the task of breaking the line of advancing Turkish ships. A very bloody battle followed. It was won by the Christians. Most of the Turkish fleet was lost. Agostino Barbarigo perished, fighting bravely, Sebastiano Venier was wounded. Meanwhile, in August, Marcantonio Bragadin, with many others, had met a horrible end at the hands of the Turks, who had not kept the terms of their surrender. The victory of Lepanto, partly on account of the diversity of the Christian allies' interests, could not be exploited and the Republic, in 1573, signed a separate Peace with the Ottomans, which formalised the loss of Cyprus, but allowed trade to be resumed with the Levant.

Venice versus Rome

The second half of the sixteenth century and the seventeenth century were characterised by the spread of the Protestant Reformation and, in the countries that remained Catholic, the beginning of that complex of political acts, religious doctrines, and consequent changes of culture and custom which was later to be known as the Counter-Reformation. One of the key moments in that long struggle was the Council of Trent (1545-1563). Venice was among the first states to accept the decrees of the Council; yet almost at once she found herself resisting the claims put forward by the Roman Curia, which had begun to give practical application, in its relations with the Catholic states, to the Tridentine formulations.

On the problems created by relations with Rome, and on other important political questions, there was considerable disagreement among the rulers of Venice about the limits of the Republic's power. Those who disagreed with what had been the traditional view were divided into two groups, which could almost be considered two parties, known as "the young" and "the old". They often had the upper hand over the traditional majority, and they were more prudent, more conservative, and more moderate.

The "old" group consisted of men who were deeply entrenched in "the establishment". As far as foreign policy was concerned they clung to "reflection", believing that by now Venice could play only a modest part in Europe and that she should maintain good relations with Rome. As to home affairs, they believed that the Senate was too big a body to handle matters of importance; they preferred the authority of smaller institutions such as the Council of Ten.

The "young" party, on the contrary, was a party of young patricians who wanted a foreign policy directed at seeking agreements with those other powers, including Protestant countries, who were interested in containing Spain and the Hapsburgs. They also believed in taking a tough line with Rome, in defence of the prerogatives of the state. As to home affairs, they were resolved to fight for the restitution of authority to important magistratures that had been deprived of it.

The powers of the Council of Ten had been the subject of disagreement for a long time. Its competence had steadily widened over the past fifty years and often encroached on that of other institutions, such as the Senate. The question came to a head in 1582-3. It was a crucial moment for the "young" party.

In 1582 it was at last possible to put together in the Great Council an opposition capable of putting a stop to the overweening power of the Council of Ten. After months of discussion a "correction" was agreed upon which delimited the competence of the Council of Ten in the fields of finance and foreign policy, and re-established the pre-eminence of the Senate.

The contention, old and new, with Rome was getting worse, meanwhile. There was endless controversy over whether Rome or Venice should have power to confer the great ecclesiastical benefices, and over the prerogative claimed by the Republic of choosing the people to propose as bishops for Venetian sees (for the most part members of the nobility). There were questions arising from the Venetian hostility to the ecclesiastical immunities (fiscal, judicial, etc.); questions arising from the administration of the sovereignty the Venetians claimed over the Adriatic, which created obstacles for the papal ships based on the port of Ancona. More recent causes of friction included the request of Clement VIII that the Patriarch of Venice, who was chosen by the Senate, should – like the other bishops – have a degree in theology or canon law and go to Rome to undergo an examination; the question of the *"marrani"*, the Spanish and Portuguese Jews compelled to become Catholics, who, in the more tolerant climate of Venice, tended to return to Judaism;

the question of the limits and controls to which the Venetian government subjected the Holy Office (that is, the Inquisition) in Veneto; and quarrels over the application of the Index of prohibited books (for one thing, Venice needed to protect her publishing industry).

In 1605 Clement VIII died and, after the brief pontificate of Leo XI, Paul V ascended the papal throne. There was no lack of motives and pretexts for settling the score with Venice; Paul V requested the repeal of laws which forbade the building of new churches, hospitals and holy places and the transfer of real estate from the secular sphere to the ecclesiastical without the Senate's authorisation. The Pope requested in addition the restitution to the ecclesiastical court of two priests responsible for serious common crimes whom the Council of Ten had had arrested and was about to judge.

The only response was the election, in January 1606, of Leonardo Donà as Doge. He was perhaps the most eminent member of the "young" party, and his election was interpreted in Rome as defiance.

In April, seeing that the Republic was not meeting his demands, Paul V delivered a "warning" which amounted to an ultimatum: if within twenty-four days the laws had not been repealed and the two imprisoned priests had not been handed over to the ecclesiastical court, the rulers of Venice would be excommunicated, and the state would be interdicted, that is, all religious functions, such as the administering of sacraments, would be forbidden. It was not the first rebuke Rome had ever inflicted on Venice, but it was certainly the most resounding.

The government countered this "warning" by having a "protest" displayed all over Veneto. It declared the papal document contrary to sacred scripture, to the Fathers of the Church, and to sacred canon law: the Venetian clergy ought not to obey it; religious functions should be carried out in the normal way. It was an open rupture between Venice and Rome. On the one side the independence of the Church from the state and the supremacy of the spiritual power over the temporal was being defended; on the other, independence from Rome was being defended, together with the state's power to control ecclesiastical institutions and subject them to conditions.

Almost all the secular clergy accepted the government's directives, while there was a certain amount of defection on the part of the religious orders, that is, among the recently founded Counter-Reformation orders such as the Jesuits, the Teatrini, etc., who preferred to leave Veneto rather than toe the authorities' line. There was undoubtedly some reluctance, some resistance and conscientious objection among the people, too, especially in rural areas, and accordingly there was some repression, but the full history of the episode is still to be written.

However, on the whole the Venetian people made common cause with the government, and this was the state's real victory.

Throughout 1606 there developed what was called the "war of the writings", that is, the publication of a great number of writings in support of Venice or Rome.

The man who supplied the ideological ammunition for the line of Venetian resistance was Brother Paolo Sarpi, who wrote the "protest". As a theologian and authority on canon law and a member of the Republic's office of Consultants in Law (which the government had used for many years), he was also the author of much more on the subject, including many consultative documents for the government.

The dispute between Venice and the Pope created international problems: Spain and the Hapsburgs of Austria were on the Pope's side; France and Protestant England and Holland supported Venice, or at least were not hostile to her. The situation was not pushed to an outcome by either party. Spain was the first to attempt mediation, but without success. A second attempt, which did succeed, was made by the French Cardinal François de Joyeuse. The compromise he arranged involved handing over the two priests charged with crimes to France (who then probably delivered them into the hands of the ecclesiastical authorities); the suspension, but not the repeal, of the laws which had been the pretext for the controversy;

and finally the simultaneous cancellation of the papal interdict and the Venetian "protest". A year had passed. It was 1607.

The war for Candia and the reconquest of Morea

In the Mediterranean (but also in the Adriatic) the corsairs represented a great problem for Venice. Piracy had been a phenomenon always and on every sea but now, in the seventeenth century, the consequences of the pirate war conducted in the Adriatic by the Uscocchi were particularly disastrous for the Venetians. The Uscocchi were Christian refugees of various nationalities and from various countries, for the most part fleeing from the Turks. They had built themselves bases on the Dalmatian coast of Quarnaro, in territories nominally controlled by Austria and Hungary.

Their pirate ships were fast, light vessels of shallow draft, and behind them there was Austria. Austria's purpose was to challenge Venetian sovereignty in the Adriatic (which was beginning to be a dead letter) and stir up trouble between the Venetians and the Turks, whose merchant ships were attacked in Adriatic waters where Turkey and Venice both claimed to guarantee safety.

To solve the problem of the Uscocchi the Republic did not hesitate to make war on Austria in the autumn of 1615, laying siege to

Gradisca. The siege dragged on without result, however, showing the military weakness of the Venetians. Venice had to accept the mediation of Spain, which achieved an end to the war without making much of a change to the situation *ante bellum*, but laying on Austria the responsibility of transferring the Uscocchi from the coast to the interior.

Before the 1630s, the Republic got involved in two other wars, the first arising from the effort of the Governor of Milan (that is, Spain) to gain control of Valtellina, the second from the struggle for the succession to the dukedom of Mantua. On both occasions Venice, having ranged herself on the side of France, found herself excluded from the peace negotiations conducted by the great powers. Her international weight was clearly not what it had been.

These ventures into warfare, from Gradisca onwards, had revealed the increasing inadequacy of the Venetian army. The political and military intentions of "the young" seemed bold and imaginative, but "the old" and their prudent assessment of the Venetian position proved to be more realistic.

The truth was, "the young" had by now exhausted the drive that had enabled them to relaunch the Republic on various planes. It reveals itself on closer inspection to be a drive that was limited by the objective impossibility of reviving the power of a state like Venice on a European scale, and by a political vision which, as Gino Benzoni points out, did not comprehend any thought of reform, any plan to update the institutional and social system inherited from the past.

The plague of 1630-31 was perhaps more terrible than that of 1575-76. Although the Commissioner for Health fought it hard, and was well equipped to do so, it left extensive demographic, economic and social destruction behind it. Another consequence was that the various elements of the Venetian ruling class all dedicated themselves to conservation and "reflection", though with plenty of inconsistencies in their views.

These inconsistencies made themselves felt in the long, long war in the hopeless defence of Candia, at least in some of its aspects and some of its phases.

In the second half of 1644 the Maltese made a foray against the Turkish fleet. It was a more serious attack than usual. The Turks thought that the Venetians were partly responsible. The Venetians believed that the affair could be settled, as usual, by diplomatic means, but, on the contrary, in the middle of 1645 the *bailo*, that is to say the Venetian ambassador to Constantinople, was arrested and the Turks invaded Candia. That was the beginning of the war, a war of besieged fortresses on the island and of supplies and strategic diversions on land and sea. (The Turkish assault in Dalmatia in 1645-48 was repulsed by the Venetians with the help of their fleet. There were Venetian sorties in the Dardanelles.) In Candia they held out, hoping for international help which did not come, except from the French and even that help was too little and too late. The war was a great haemorrhage of ships, men and above all money. After twenty-four years of it (in Candia only three or four thousand Venetian men survived unharmed) Francesco Morosini, who had taken over the command of the naval forces, had no alternative but to negotiate a peace, in 1669, which meant surrendering the island, although on formally honourable terms.

With the fall of Candia, it seemed that the centuries-old adventure of the "sea state" of Venice in the Levant was over, except that a complex of international circumstances allowed the Republic to get the Morea back.

The Turks, round about the 1670s, had lost control of Hungary under pressure from Austria. In 1683 they attempted to strike back, aiming their attack at central Europe. They nearly reached Vienna, but the Austrians, with the aid of the allied armies of the Catholic countries, launched a victorious counter-offensive which put Hungary and Transylvania under the control of the Hapsburgs. Venice joined the "Holy League" of Austria, Poland and the Pope against the Turks in 1684, and, with Francesco Morosini as commander, embarked on a series of successful expeditions by land and sea, which led to her conquest of most of the Morea, that is, the Peloponese. The Treaty of Carlowitz (1699), which closed the cycle of wars, confirmed those Venetian conquests. This time the Republic showed that she wanted to treat the "sea state" differently from before, in the sense that she tried to make an effort at "modern" organization in administering the territories, by compiling a land register, dividing territory into interconnected administrative districts, and programming agricultural and economic development. For the most part, however, it was only a matter of programming. In 1714 the Turks attacked again and, while the Austrians were victorious at Petercaradino and Belgrade, the Venetians were turned out of the Morea with the greatest ease. (Some of her troops did not put up a fight, and the Greek population was hostile.) With the Peace of Passarowitz (1718) Venice was compelled to give up her presence in the Levant, and the possessions of the "sea state" were reduced, until the end of the Republic, to those in Istria, Dalmatia, the Ionic islands and a few scraps of land in Albania.

In the course of the seventeenth century Venice ceased to be the great Mediterranean centre of commercial exchange that she had been in the past; she found great difficulty in fitting out merchant ships; she suffered from the competition offered by the French, the English and the Dutch. Faced with the enormous economic and commercial development of each of the modern states, the old Venetian port was reduced to the more modest functions of a port supplying its own region with provisions for a populous city and raw materials for her industries and those of the Venetian *terraferma*, and the transit of goods to and from the Po (and to some extent German) hinterland.

Eighteenth-century senescence

The policies of neutrality and conservation originated in the sixteenth and seventeenth centuries but were not pursued consistently until the eighteenth. By that time the rulers of Venice were more fully aware that they were the right policies to follow, partly because the survival of the Venetian state required it.

Notwithstanding pressures and flattery, the Republic did not allow herself to be involved in either of the European alliances which throughout the first half of the century fought each other in endless wars. These were fought in Italy as well as elsewhere, sometimes even on Venetian soil, in spite of Venetian neutrality, at first over the Spanish succession, then over the Polish and then, in the forties, over the Austrian.

Later Venice resisted Catherine II of Russia's suggestion that she should try to get back her possessions in the Levant. From 1768 to 1774 Catherine fought victorious campaigns against the Turks, not only on land but also with fleets sent from the Baltic to the Mediterranean.

The Senate also refused to let naval actions against pirates turn into war. Venice tackled the barbarian territories of Tripoli, Algeria and Tunisia in 1766 and 1767 and then again in 1784-92 in exhausting campaigns fought by the naval squadrons of Angelo Emo, but even in such places as these the Senate had no intention of embarking on out-and-out war.

It was true that a policy of neutrality offered a less and less reliable guarantee of safety. The example of the partition of Poland in 1772 had demonstrated that the dismemberment of small states to allow reciprocal rewards for the great powers had to be reckoned with, as a feature of international politics. But it was still true that Venetian neutrality, "impartiality" towards the European alignments, especially the French and Austrian, was an ineluctable policy, and felt as such by the rulers of Venice – and often by foreign observers, too.

An ineluctable policy, and also a policy closely connected with that other policy of rigid conservatism towards the institutions of the state. They were two fundamental and interdependent policies, which between them determined many of the original characteristics of the political, social and cultural life of the eighteenth-century Veneto, and many of the inconsistencies suffered and meekly swallowed by the rulers of Venice, and the ruled, in the remaining scrap of the Republic's life.

By means of a process which began in previous centuries, the distribution of real power between the patricians in the eighteenth century was organized as various levels of authority. There was a relatively restricted group of elevated and not-so-elevated patrician "houses" known as "the great". They virtually dominated the government; that is, they enjoyed permanent control of the decisive organisms of power such as the Council of Ten, the *Signoria*, the Senate and the College (the steering committee of the Senate). A second, numerous group of "houses" - middle and lower-middle (*"i quarantiotti"*, the Fortyers) found a place in state organisms of middling importance, such as "the Forties"; and finally other patricians, decidedly poor in financial terms (and they were the majority) divided the minor offices between them, and national assistance too.

The most evident inconsistencies faced by the élite of the Venetian patrician class in the second half of the eighteenth century were those relating to the development of policies which on the one hand guaranteed conservation, *en bloc* and in detail, to the institutions inherited from the distant past and, on the other hand, were sufficiently open to the influence of the times to allow the introduction of moderate changes. Such changes affected the functioning of the economy and the administration, as seen in the reforms currently taking place in European states ruled by Enlightened Absolutism (Austria, Tuscany ...), if not in the more radical feelings and propositions of the Enlightenment.

At the beginning of the sixties a group of patricians led by Angelo Querini pointed out one of these inconsistencies and made a considerable stir. In the eighties another group, led by Giorgio Pisani and Carlo Contarini, drew attention to another. These men presented themselves as "innovators", but in reality they were explicitly fighting not for some change to the institutions of state (for example, involvement in managing the power to represent the non-patrician social strata and the "sea state" and "land state"), but for a return to a more or less mythical past, in which – so said these innovators – there had been a more equitable distribution of power among the great constitutional organisms (meaning among the Venetian patricians).

The conflicts between Angelo Querini, Giorgio Pisani and Carlo Contarini ended with their arrest and banishment. That way of silencing opposition, that disproportionate and fearful reaction of the establishment was the sign of inflexibility, of an almost uncritical conditioned reflex, which seized the Venetian patricians whenever they suspected a challenge to the constitutional *status quo*, even when the challenge came from within the system.

However, an authoritative group of patricians (their most important leader was Andrea Tron) showed initiative when there was a possibility of reforming the political and social institutions in ways which did not seem revolutionary, but on the contrary conducive to reinforcing their durability. It was thus that in the second half of the eighteenth century there were momentous reforms in ecclesiastical organisations: better control of the secular clergy, a great reduction in the number of monks and nuns, suppression of some monasteries and convents and extensive appropriation of ecclesiastical property by the state. In the field of public finance, state budgets were introduced for the first time. (The policy of neutrality combined with an effort lasting many years had made it possible to absorb the deficits caused by the wars of the past.) Social, economic and demographic statistics were compiled for the state's population register. Measures for restructuring maritime trade and the port of Venice were introduced, and a very advanced Code of the Venetian merchant navy. Much was said and a certain amount done about the unification and modernisation of harbour dues, customs duties and so on. Plans were made to compile collections of laws, and certain innovations in methods of sentencing were proposed. Hitherto it had been possible (in the city of Venice as distinct from the rest of the Venetian state) for the government to make use of a *ius proprium*, which took precedence over the common law and administered justice through judges who were members of the sovereign political body. Measures were sought, and studies requested, for the relaunching of agriculture and manufacture and the up-dating of their technology. In the vast world of

Venetian guilds there was a call for new openings and also for closures. The education system was effectively reformed. An impressive welfare network had been inherited from the past and it was now suggested that it could be improved by new initiatives including a People's Home for the poor. Studies and plans for remedying the degeneration of land and roads were brought up to date, but, as things turned out, it was only in the city of Venice that any real effort was made to carry them out, in the construction of the *"murazzi"*, the stout sea defences of the lagoon. There was an attempt at modernising the ramshackle military forces (the military college of Verona) and other reforms too were discussed.

As Franco Venturi has recently pointed out, the politicians' programmes of reform were accompanied (with or without any connection) by cultural discussion in, for example, the *Journal of Italy regarding natural science and principally agriculture, the arts and commerce.*

In comparison with what was planned, very little, to tell the truth, was actually done, but discussion of reform was widespread and uninhibited. In the archives there are documents that are of great value to historians: records of the reform commissions which, sector by sector, tried to reconstruct the history of the economic and social institutions of the Republic and to show what they were like in the eighteenth century; they set out to plan and propose changes and modernisations of those very institutions, not to replace them, and with what was left over from activity abroad.

Eighteenth-century Venice was the capital of a state which, with the institutional and social identity imprinted on her in the middle ages, had lived through the modern age; the capital of a state that was old and weak, but in which good sense in political management was not diminished in spite of age and weakness. Illusory and fanciful destinies were neither proposed nor imposed. Perhaps it was partly for this reason that the city, in its social aspect, gave the impression that her inhabitants, whether citizens or foreigners, enjoyed a free, relaxed daily life that flowed peacefully yet festively, bright with vitality.

In the second half of the eighteenth century the population of the city was about 140,000 while that of the entire state was about 2,860,000.

The end of the Republic and the democratic Municipality of 1797

The French Revolution set in motion the events that were to carry the old Venetian state out of history.

After it became clear that the revolution had succeeded in '89-90, Venice continued her policy of standing equidistant from France and Austria and did not enter the first anti-French coalition; on the contrary, she tried as hard to overcome every difficulty that stood in the way of re-establishing diplomatic relations with France as the changes in that country's institutions required.

Naturally, above all after '93, the Venetian government intensified its vigilance against the dangers of a massive infiltration of revolutionary ideas. Alarm and repression were out of all proportion to the size of the little groups who were anxious for changes in the institutions which were so weak in the Venetian state.

In 1795, when year III of the revolutionary period ended with the proclamation of the constitution, the government of the Directoire was established in France. The country found itself still at war with the rest of the first coalition. The most important front was in Germany, on the Rhine. It was decided, at the end of the year, to transform the Italian front into a real second front. The general appointed to command the army that was raised to fight in Italy was the young Napoleon Bonaparte.

From January 1796 the Venetian representative in Paris, Alvise Querini, began to keep Venice informed of the French preparations for war. His dispatches were very intelligent and lucid, like those of his predecessors Almorò Pisani and Antonio Capello, who had forecast, described and interpreted the revolutionary events of the preceding years. Diplomacy had always been a strong point of the Venetians (centuries of European history are to be found in the dispatches and reports of Venetian ambassadors).

In the spring of 1796 the French armies who had entered Italy defeated the Piedmontese, attacked Austrian Lombardy and occupied Milan. The Austrians dug themselves in at Mantua and began to flood over Veneto. The Republic declared its neutrality, but it could not prevent the Austrians, as they retreated, or the French as they pursued them, from entering Venetian territory.

In August and September Italy was inundated with fresh Austrian armies, which Napoleon almost routinely defeated. The Veronese region, the Trentino and the Brenta valley were the chief theatres of war: there were battles at Bassano, Primolano and Friuli. At the end of the year, and then in the early months of 1797, on the strength of battles fought and won (Mantua, which had been besieged, fell on 2nd February), Napoleon won the military and political advantage that allowed him to treat with the Austrians at Leoben (18th April) for the preliminaries to peace, which, among other things, provided, in secret clauses, for territorial compensation to be made at the expense of the Republic.

The treaty was discussed in Venice in all the most important councils. There was no lack of people who thought about a pro-Austrian policy opposed to the settlement, or of those who were on the whole inclined to favour a pro-French policy. All the same, the greater part of the numerous ruling class understood the situation, with varying degrees of clarity, more or less in these terms: the Republic, regardless of any comparison with the new France, was incurably old; the survival of Venice depended on the balance of power in Europe, and that was now gone, leaving Austria and France eager to make themselves masters of Venice's remains, whether in the guise of ally and protector or in that of enemy; all resistance, therefore, was useless: it would only bring death and destruction.

In Veneto, meanwhile, the people were living through terrible experiences: their property was requisitioned (though paid for); their food was taken to provision the invading army, who committed violent outrage of all kinds; and they had to endure the arrogance of Napoleon, who received the Venetian representatives with abuse and bad manners that, even before making them angry, astounded them, making them feel the irremediable distance separating the old world, which *they* belonged to, from the new world the invaders had brought from France.

In the cities on the Lombard side of the Venetian state, at Bergamo on 12-13th March 1797, at Brescia on 17-18th March; at Salò on 25th March and at Crema on 27th, small groups of local worthies, covered by the French, took over the government of the cities, setting up democratic municipalities. They were ex-nobles, men of business and professional men, some of them with property and some of them intellectuals, including a few priests.

The Venetian Rectors of the cities hurriedly surrendered, but when the leaders of the municipalities of Brescia and Bergamo appeared in the valleys and the countryside to democratise them, the peasants opposed them and with the emblem of St Mark, cut out of posters and stuck on their caps, chased them away and began to resist the French too.

After the preliminary peace talks in Leoben, Napoleon needed a free hand. In order to make war on the Republic he had recourse to provocation and pretexts: a false proclamation signed by the Venetian *Provveditore* of the *terraferma*, urging resistance to the French; the killing of the consul of France at Zante; the insurrection of Verona against Napoleon's troops between 17th and 25th April; the sinking of the vessel *Libérateur d'Italie* which had tried to force a way into the port of the Lido. At last, on 1st May, he succeeded in declaring war.

After the Veronese rebels had been obliged to surrender, and a democratic municipality had been set up in Verona, the peasant militias of Vicenza (for the most part from the Seven *Comuni*) who had come to the help of the Veronese, dispersed. On the evening of 26th April the Venetian Rector of Vicenza left the city alone, on foot, and walked towards Padua. In Vicenza, on 27th April, the French entered the city and set up a democratic municipality.

On 28th April it was Padua's turn. All the cities and towns of Veneto were covered with a fine network of provisional democratic municipalities.

Between the 1st and the 12 May 1797 there was a continuous feverish attempt to negotiate the end of the business. Napoleon had to be treated with wherever he could be found: in Padua, it might be, with General Victor; with the Commander of the French at Mestre; with the emaciated little group of so-called Venetian "Jacobins" (their meeting centre was the Ferratini house at San Polo); with the secretary of the French Embassy in Venice, Giuseppe Villetard.

At last 12th May arrived. At break of day Andrea Spada (an ex-customs officer who was one of the leaders of the democrats) sent a note to the Great Council, which had met for the purpose of reaching a decision. In it he summarised the conditions communicated by Napoleon's headquarters in Milan. The demands were short and sharp: the installation of a representative government in Venice was indispensable; such a government could not be combined with a patrician class; Bonaparte wanted democracy to be established without delay; if the Venetians did not do it, the French would come and do it for them.

While one of the members of the Great Council was expounding the ultimatum, somewhat verbosely, to his colleagues, from outside, from the Piazzetta di S. Marco where the troops recruited by Schiavoni were embarking, came the sound of a fusillade of musketry, which they fired by way of salute to the city. It was enough to throw everyone into a panic. The councillors shouted, "That's enough! That's enough! Be gone!" The decree was put to the vote and was approved by a majority of more than five hundred. Thus did the patrician ruling class "adopt the system of the proposed provisional representative government", bringing to an end a state that was almost a thousand years old.

Power was formally handed over to the new municipality by the old patrician government with an exchange of declarations. The new government was organized in the same way as the new democratic municipalities of the *terraferma*, with an assembly of about sixty members and eight committees: Public Welfare; the Military; Health; Finance and the Mint; Shipbuilding and the Navy; Banks, Commerce and Guilds; Grants and Benefits; Education.

The political and social climate of the summer of 1797 in the towns and cities of Veneto was extraordinary. It was a climate of new possibilities, freedom of discussion, effervescence, search for identity on the part of various groups of the population, visions of what power could mean. There were constant meetings of the assembly, public and otherwise; meetings of the committees; speeches in the various tribunes; newspapers, pamphlets,

proclamations; patriotic theatrical perfor-
mances, huge placards painted with patriotic
pictures and captions; ritualised trees of liberty; a revival of symbols and names; it was in
part the culture of politics, in part the politics
of culture, in part a cultural revolution. There
was furious and wide-ranging debate, comparable with many in the past and, still more,
with those that would later be created by the
advent of the Austrians. A lot of changes had to
be made in many branches of administration
(public finance, justice, the political represen-
tation of the people, ...), and there was a lot of
ideological and philosophical discussion. In a
very short time an enormous quantity of pamphlets, minutes of municipality meetings and
newspapers had accumulated. Debate was
more than ample, even if it was for the most
part nourished and guided in a moderate direction by the middle classes who, on the whole,
left their imprint on municipal power, showing
that they had learnt a considerable amount of
administrative and political know-how from
the model provided by the revolutionary
French in '95. Here and there, there was a
debate raised by the contributions, at times
very significant, of intellectuals of a new stamp,
such as Ugo Foscolo or Vincenzo Dandolo, who
were to animate the public education societies
(Venetian education was important) as centres
of relatively radical political and cultural agita-
tion, inspired by the premises of the
Enlightenment and the principles of '89.

On 17th October, at Campoformio (or rather, at Passariano) a peace treaty was signed between Napoleon and Austria. Austria received Veneto, Istria and Dalmatia, while Bergamo, Brescia and Crema were handed over to the Cisalpine Republic (recognised by Austria). France took the Ionic islands and a certain amount of Albanian territory which had belonged to the Venetian Republic.

It was the end of independence for Venice and Veneto.

The nineteenth century and foreign domination: Austria - Napoleon - Austria

With the events of 1797 the Venetian state made its exit from history. Venice became simply a city involved in the affairs of other states.

On 18th January 1798 the first units of the army of occupation settled down in the city. After a brief period of transition, an Imperial government answerable to Vienna was set up. Leading members of the one-time patrician class and of the one-time democratic municipality were absorbed into the new administration. In the brief interlude of democratic government that the various sectors of the population had enjoyed in 1797, they had glimpsed the possible realisation of social and political aspirations, but the absolutist Austrian system put an end to that. In 1800 Venice hosted the long conclave which ended with the election of

Pope Pius VII.

Only after 1803 did Vienna proceed to a more clearly defined administrative system in the Venetian provinces, partly because the political and military climate of Italy was uncertain; but at the end of 1805 and the beginning of 1806, in accordance with the Treaty of Presburg (which sealed a series of French victories over the Austrians), Veneto became part of Napoleon's Kingdom of Italy, of which Milan was the capital. Napoleon had proclaimed himself not only Emperor of the French but also King of Italy, in 1803.

During the first decade of the century a series of big changes were made in the economic administration of Venice: there was development of the free port, the Arsenal (shipyard), the port services and the lagoon defences; the Chamber of Commerce was relaunched and public funding was increased. The city buildings were also extensively altered: some were demolished, others gutted, palaces were prepared for public receptions, gardens and open spaces were created and adorned with monumental statues. The ancient system of public assistance was liquidated, as were the corporate institutions and the ecclesiastical, too, in part. It was an important moment for neoclassicism (Canova, at least, must be mentioned). Venice and Veneto now began to have experience of contact with a modern system of government – watchful, aware of what was going on, in control – an experience that was part good and part bad. To be subject to military conscription was traumatic, especially for those who found themselves having to pay in their own person for someone else's military glory.

After Napoleon's disastrous Russian campaign, the political and military situation was changed in Italy, as elsewhere. For the nth time, Venetian territory became a theatre of war. Between October 1813 and April 1814 Venice was besieged from the sea by the English and on land by the Austrians. When Napoleon's armies were dispersed everywhere, following the Congress of Vienna in 1815, Veneto became once more an Austrian province.

Between 1815 and 1866 Venice was part of the Kingdom of Lombardy-Veneto, ruled by two Governors who presided over government Colleges, one in Milan and one in Venice, under the Austrian crown. Many of the administrative and economic institutions introduced by the Napoleonic government continued. Primary education improved. The economy grew, particularly in Lombardy, in spite of strong fiscal pressure. Although centralisation in Vienna increased, at local level the bureaucracy made further strides towards a modern and functional organisation of men and things. Venice was constantly given objectives for development, and if, in the first twenty years, social conditions became much worse, with a marked demographic decline, increased unemployment and poverty, impoverishment of industry and crafts, reduction of construction work and shipbuilding, from the end of the thirties the city's economy began to look up. The free port was extended, important public works were undertaken (for example, the infrastructure of the port), the railway bridge across the lagoon was begun in 1846, and tourism continued to make quite a considerable contribution to the city's prosperity. In 1847 the ninth Congress of Italian Scientists was held in Venice. In some ways it was a defiance of Austria and a celebration of the lost independence of the Venetian Republic.

Although several middle-class groups were amassing substantial fortunes and setting themselves up as financiers, no broad-based and enterprising middle class, conscious of itself, emerged. Perhaps partly for this reason, political opposition to the state of things was weaker in Venice than elsewhere. All the same, when an opportunity arose for a general Italian and European movement of rebellion, with the watchword "national independence", a considerable number of landowners, professional men, intellectuals and patriots, supported by substantial numbers of the common people, was able, in March 1848, to overcome the armed forces and the Austrian administration, proclaim the Republic (with Daniele Manin at the head of it) and direct it with moderation for more than a year. In the last few months the city was under siege and, after desperate resistance, surrendered in August 1849.

After the months of rebellion in 1848-9, Venice was once more brought to heel by Austria. There was a period of deep depression, followed in the fifties by a degree of recovery. The hopes raised by the second war of independence and by the victories of Napoleon III and the Piedmontese over the Austrians were dashed by the sudden ending of the conflict, which gave Lombardy to the French but left Veneto in the hands of the Austrians.

Venice had to wait for years for the third war of independence, years in which foreign struggles for possession of Veneto and repression of the Venetians became ever more violent. At last, in 1866, thanks to French victories, the city, together with the whole Veneto region, was ceded to Napoleon III and by him handed over to the Kingdom of Italy, which had been proclaimed in 1860. The population of the city had fallen, at that date, to something less than 130,000.

In the kingdom of Italy

The first twenty "Italian" years of the municipal administration of Venice were given their particular character by officials who were moderate and conservative men and who did not succeed in improving the depressing economic lot of the city, although they worked hard to relaunch the fortunes of the port and to encourage industrialisation. They continued the rearrangement of the city, and also the havoc that had previously been wrought there, in the name of improving roads and dwellings, just as they continued the impoverishment (removal and sale) of the immense resources of books, documents and works of art accumulated in the years of the Republic, an impoverishment to which, in the era of Napoleonic and Austrian domination, both rulers and private citizens had contributed and to which the latter continued to contribute.

After the nineties, thanks in part to agreements that encouraged changes, the left-wing liberals and the radicals (such as the mayor, Riccardo Selvatico) began to establish their influence. It was they who launched the regulating plan of 1891 and programmes for commercial and industrial development, for the secularisation of schools and social welfare services, for the democratisation of some processes of local administration, for the development of professional training schools, for the definition and development of the health services, and for "healthy and economical housing for the people". As opponents they had conservatives and clerics, who resented, among other things, the endorsement the municipal authorities gave to their experiments in mayoral organization, which had a socialist tinge. (In 1892, the year in which the Italian Socialist Party was founded, the Chamber of Labour was opened in Venice.)

With Crispi in power in the central government, the progressive local government (*giun-ta*) of Venice had a hard time. Before long it was possible for a group formed by under-standings between clerics and moderates and encouraged by Giuseppe Sarto, nominated Patriarch of the city in 1894, to beat the "popu-lar" party (made up of left-wing liberals and supporters of democracy), which they did in 1895, and to be elected as a *giunta* which would succeed in hanging on to power for twenty years as governors of the *comune*, with Filippo Grimani as mayor. The other important event of the year 1895 was the inauguration of the International Art Exhibition which was later to be known as the Biennale.

In the decades in which they were in power, this *giunta* representing clerical and moderate interests set on foot plans for an industrial area at Marghera, the development of the Lido as a seaside resort and the doubling of the lagoon bridge. They also introduced pub-lic transport run by the municipality *(vaporetti)* and certain services (gas and electricity) under joint public and private ownership. Chief among the private investors in the latter enter-prise was the electricity group (Celina, Sade) with international, Italian and Venetian capital, whose great patron was to be, on account of his economic and political influence in Venice and Veneto, Giuseppe Volpi.

The war of colonial conquest in Libya aroused opposition among politicians all over the country, including Venice. The hypothesis of an alliance of Democrats and Radicals with the Socialists faded, and its place was taken by nationalist groups, of whom some saw the possibility of joining forces with the programmes of the Catholics and the Liberal Conservatives.

The Great War of 1914-18 was particularly difficult for Venice and Veneto, on account of evacuation, bombardment and negative repercussions both economic and social. However, it did not greatly impede the realisation of plans which had been made before the war and were carried out after it. Work on the industrialisation of Portomarghera began in 1917: development of the port, the industrial area and the residential quarter. It was to continue to grow hugely during the twenties and then in the late thirties and again with the outbreak of the second world war in '39. From the point of view of social involvement (the creation of jobs) the Portomarghera enterprise aimed deliberately at serving the interests of the hinterland and remained rather remote from Venice, where local industry continued to decline and only the port remained important as a source of work.

In the twenties, fascism dominated the whole country and demolished every other political force and, in addition, the workers' organisations, including the so-called "white" organisations, which, besides being Catholic, were strong and democratic in Veneto. Active anti-fascist cells (those belonging to the Communist Party and created at Livorno in

1921 were particularly dedicated) offered resistance in Venice, too, and not a few were persecuted. Meanwhile (in 1933) a road bridge for motor traffic was built beside the railway bridge across the lagoon.

With the partisan rising and the surrender of the German garrison, Venice was liberated from the Nazi-Fascists between 26th and 28th April 1945. The resistance movement had fought hard in Veneto, and dramatic episodes had also taken place in Venice which, however, unlike Portomarghera and Mestre, had been almost entirely spared by air raids.

From the post-war period to the present day

Once reconstruction had started, and after a brief period of administration by the Left, the city, until the mid-fifties, was governed without interruption by Catholic politicians supported by the capitalist and business worlds (in part, the worlds that had supported Fascism). They were firmly rooted in the middle classes, but their dominance was modified by a strong left-wing faction within the Christian Democrat party and by contacts with the Socialists that led, finally, in the sixties, to explicit agreements with them to govern the city jointly. After the troubles of '68 (including a particularly violent disturbance at the Biennale), the Left began to move slowly towards the Communists. A *giunta* of the Left came to power in the 1975 elections, and remained there until 1990, with first a Socialist as mayor and then a Republican. During that period there was one short interval, from the 1985 elections until 1988, in which the *giunta* in power consisted of the Centre Left and Christian Democrats (The latter always controlled the regional *giunta*.)

After the war the economic and urban development of Marghera and Mestre was similar to that of the other industrial areas of northern Italy and independent of Venice. Venice, meanwhile, had problems deriving from government that was lacking or distorted or void of vision, and they got steadily worse. That government's characteristics were related to the city's history and topography, and the problems were determined first by the application of the "industrialist" ideology to the *terraferma* and later (in the sixties) by the development of the city's economy almost uniquely in the direction of tourism. This narrow specialism accentuated the decadence of the few other traditional industrial activities that remained, such as shipbuilding. Other problems concerned profound inconsistencies in the housing market, in which non-residents played a significant part; and there were problems about alterations in the ecosystem of the lagoon (resulting in part from digging the deep canal between Malamocco and Portomarghera for oil-tankers, of subsidence and high tides, among them the disastrous one of 1966, etc.); problems about conservation of the city, in

spite of noteworthy efforts at recovery and protection, partly forced on the government by
UNESCO's interventions and those of foreign
associations; the problems of air and water pol-
lution producing rapid and very obvious damage, of the damage done by the swell produced
by motor boats, excessive loads of visitors, etc.
As a consequence of all these problems, the
population became older and smaller: in 1945
there were 178,000 inhabitants, in 1960 there
were 145,500 and by May 1990 it had fallen to
78,900.

The national parliament approved a "special" law for the protection of Venice in 1973
and, the following year, by a unanimous vote,
the Council of the *comune* put it into effect,
with detailed plans. Overlapping fields of competence, fluctuating public and private interest
(often in conflict with one another), anxiety not
to lose the opportunities offered by such an
unusual project, ended by thwarting the enthu-
siasm for tackling it and effectiveness in doing
so, which were perfectly possible on the techni-
cal plane, and obligatory, considering the grav-
ity of the problems.

The increase in the size of the difficulties
has had the effect of convincing people that
only some extraordinary intervention can
"save" Venice. This is true, but it is in danger of
obscuring the other essential thing to be considered, which is the ordinary conduct of daily
life. Thus, while impressive plans are made to
tackle problems concerning water, the deterio-

ration of the banks of the lagoon continues, and since the fifties and sixties the normal cleaning of the *rii*, the narrow canals in the city, which was carried out uninterruptedly for centuries, has stopped. The lagoon system, too, needs to be worked as it used to be; it is an enormous, natural purifying plant and it therefore needs the regular removal of mud.

The sum total of small, almost unnoticeable daily facts ends by being both conclusive and overlooked. And in the last few years the ordinary facts of daily life have been in danger of telling the city's story. To give just one example, when two young people get married they have to leave the historic centre of the city and, in order to raise a family, look for somewhere to live in the hinterland, given the situation in the housing market; and even if one marriage does not make a great difference, the phenomenon as a whole has a very great effect, not only on the demographic decline but also, and worse, on the unnatural ageing of a population which sees fewer and fewer babies born. The close interconnections originating from the courses agreed on (whether made or never put into practice) and the complex characteristics of modern life gradually give way to an alteration of its structure.

In some ways Venice takes her exceptionalness for granted; people who over-emphasise it miss the true reasons for it, chief among them the fact that such a place still contains the rhythms of life and has not become simply the home of museums. From this point of view, in a historical perspective, the final fact to point out is perhaps a process of "neighbourhoodization", whereby the historic centre (and the whole of the lagoon area) is given up to certain functions (in general, not very highly developed service functions), while the business of living has left it. This is in danger of depriving Venice of the character of a true city; a true city can only live on the sum total of its diverse functions.

However, one constant element of the whole Venetian story, persisting among its highs and lows, its splendours and miseries, has been that of finding the energy and the ability to get out of the most complex predicaments. In any case, the "problem" of Venice remains, as is well known, open. In some ways, one might say, desperately open.

Printed by Industrie Grafiche Pacini Editore S.p.A.
Via A. Gherardesca • 56121 Ospedaletto • Pisa (Italy)
Tel. +39050313011 • Fax +390503130300
Internet: http://www.pacinieditore.it
July 2001